About the author

Lucy met Howard back when they were both 17, and a mere eight years later he got down on one knee on a warm autumn evening in Portugal and asked her to marry him. She said yes, triggering a frenzied eleven months of dress-picking, detail-planning, lavender-planting (more on that later), décor-arranging, favour-making . . .

Her friends and family called her Bridezilla – she just thought she was organised. Lucy loved getting married (in a marquee in Hertfordshire, on a day that, after almost a year of worrying, turned out to be the only dry day in August). Over the past year she has loved diving back into wed-world for this, her fifth book.

Lucy is a journalist at the *Evening Standard*, for whom her work has won a series of awards including business journalist of the year. She is the author of four previous books including *Ausperity: live the life you want for less* (Heron) and *Entrepreneur* (Capstone).

lucytobin.com   Twitter @lucytobin

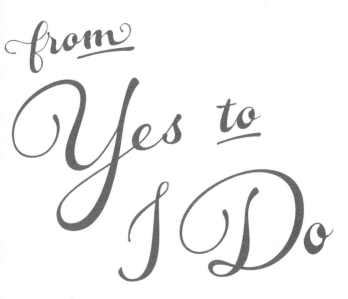

from Yes to I Do

THE WEDDING GUIDE FOR A MODERN BRIDE

LUCY TOBIN

First published in Great Britain in 2014 by Heron Books
an imprint of

Quercus Editions
55 Baker Street
7th Floor, South Block
London W1U 8EW

A CIP catalogue record for this book is available
from the British Library

HB ISBN 978 1 78206 671 2
EBOOK ISBN 978 1 78206 672 9

10 9 8 7 6 5 4 3 2 1

Printed and bound in Hong Kong by Hung Hing

Designed by Bob Vickers

Dedication

This book is for everyone who helped make our wedding day the best day of our lives.

But especially to my mum: thank you for the endless hours of dress-trials, lavender-gardening, research and wed-chats – and for everything. And to Dad: thank you for your Offley maps and cabling and proofreading and for your lovely speech.

To Clare and David, thank you for registrar-ing and for ribbons and for all your help and support.

Rob, thank you for brilliant MC-ing, and to Anna and my friends, thank you for such a brilliant hen weekend.

And to Howard . . . thanks for asking. Still can't believe we're married!

Contents

Dietary requirements 149

Cheers! 165

RSVP 173

Flower power 193

Intro

from Yes to I Do

Why read this book?

It's an all-day celebration where every minute is filled with the people, music, food and drink that you love most. You're surrounded by your best friends and closest family. Everyone there wants you to have the most amazing day of your life, and will move mountains

– or at least tables and chairs around the venue – to ensure that happens. So surely planning your wedding should be a whole lot of fun?

And it is – but most brides (and the few blokes out there who join their fiancées in more planning than just attending the wine-tasting) also find big-day-making to be one of the most stressful times of their lives. Parents fall out, friends turn into enemies, the groom that you want to spend the rest of your life with seems to think watching the football is more important than working out the style of your aisle, or doing anything connected to the big day, really. And you become that person you swore, over endless episodes of *Don't Tell the Bride*, that you'd never be. Yup, you're Bridezilla.

Why does it end up like this? Well, we can lay some of the blame on the booming wedding industry. Britain's nuptials industry is valued at around £10 billion and even has its own award ceremonies where suppliers toast their success in getting Britain's brides and grooms to part with their cash – and sometimes their sanity – for services most nearly-weds hadn't even known existed.

Yet no bride-and-groom-shaped vodka luge will guarantee a long and happy marriage. If you still need convincing that you don't need to spend a lot of time or money to have a great day, think of the average success of a celebrity marriage. Kim Kardashian's wedding to

Kris Humphries cost $10 million . . . and their marriage lasted only 72 days, which works out at around $138,900 for each day of married life together.

It's not just the expense of a wedding day that can send the average bride gaga faster than she can say 'I do', it's also the fact that, before waltzing down the aisle, a lot of brides find themselves yanked in every possible direction by people stretching from Great-Aunt Dolly to the soon-to-be in-laws who you're desperate not to upset – but who you also don't want taking over your big day.

A friend of mine got engaged and, bouncing around in happiness with her other half, decided that they wanted a small do – just with family and friends, kept fairly shoestring so they could save up for a mortgage. Then her prospective mother-in-law let slip that she had already invited her ex-hairdresser, her husband's boss's daughter – oh, and her dog's best friend's dad. It's no wonder my friend felt a little strained.

Then there's the pressure to be original. Most of our parents' generation didn't feel this pressure. I blame Facebook. After years of going to friends' weddings, and seeing their snaps plastered over the social netosphere, many of us feel keen to make our day different, with favours or food stands that no one's ever seen before, or entirely home-made catering, or getting a personal wedding hashtag trending – anything to make the wedding the one that everyone talks about and dominating news feeds the next day. Sometimes we just put the pressure on ourselves, and it seems like there's one helluva lot of wedding planning to pack into a few short months.

But this book is about to make your life a whole lot easier. The single most stressful part of organising a wedding is that there seems to be so much to do. You're not entirely confident about the legal stuff about getting married, or perhaps you feel like you've forgotten something crucial – though you're not quite sure what it is. On the following pages, you'll find details of every bit of a wedding day that you could possibly want to include in your own, so you can pick and choose the bits you'd like. Like a maid of honour – but one who will *never* get sick of wed-chat and handing out advice. This book will not only help you decide how you want your big day to be, but also how to get it all organised.

In the lead-up to my wedding last summer, I had shouty days and happy days, mad days and disorganised days, and I spent most of my time at work (sorry, boss) surfing hundreds of wedding blogs to check out what everyone else was doing. Two rooms of my flat were devoted to making little lavender pots for guests and trying to grapple with a table plan. Then when it was all over, and we'd unwrapped every bit of our gift list after the big day, my (it still sounds odd) husband

and I started talking to recently married friends who revealed they'd all gone through the same dilemmas and organisational confusion.

At the same time, most of us got wed just as the UK's economy plunged into recession faster than a hard-hurled bridal bouquet. We had learnt that just because you may be budgeted-restrained, doesn't mean you have to hold back.

And that's where this book came to life. Some fellow newly-weds and I spoke to all of the caterers, venues, florists and everyone that helped us make our days, delved through our notes, remembered some of our successes and plenty of our mistakes, and together edited down what you really need to know about getting hitched – and how to have a fun and relaxing time doing it. I've also included a list of the coolest blogs and websites you can visit to inspire you along the way. Inside this book you'll find a step-by-step guide to organising every part of your big day, from the second you say 'yes' until hours after you say 'I do'.

This book is packed full of ideas for home-made details, because, as one friend puts it, 'after a year's planning for my winter wedding, designing invites, testing menus, working out which flowers were in season when, and planning things to do for the kids, the things our guests kept talking about after the big day were the DIY ideas: the photos we dotted around our venue, and the scrapbook guest book I made with friends.'

Also throughout the book there are top tips from the experts – photographers and caterers, DJs and wedding planners – who have provided handy checklists you can take along to meetings with your suppliers so you don't get duped. They also reveal where you can get away with cutting costs – just don't tell their clients that you've secured their know-how for a confetti-sized fraction of the price!

So pour a glass of something bubbly, sit back and relax. Laugh over wedding stories like the one about the ushers who had to dash around to neighbours' kitchens to heat the main dishes after a power failure at the reception. Everyone had a fab time eating by candlelight and the whole drama made for a memorable day. All weddings are wonderful. However mad, scary or bad it may feel at the planning stage, however many rain showers come or wardrobe malfunctions occur, the sheer joy of the day overcomes them all in the end.

Here's how to enjoy the journey.

What is a wedding?

I saw this listed on the first page of a Q and A on a wedding website, and laughed as it went on to explain, literally, what a wedding was, and then discuss the 'reasons why people get married'. The answers it gave, by the way, were 'love', 'social acceptance' and . . . 'the benefits of a dual-income household . . .' Hmm!

I'm definitely not going to outline what a wedding is here, but I just put the question in because it's a useful reminder on those days when the planning gets stressful, or your fiancé(e) isn't helping AT ALL, that there is a reason why you're getting married. OK, so it might possibly be social acceptance or 'the benefits of a dual-income household', but it's most likely to be because you love someone so much you want to spend the rest of your life with them. So if at some point you feel like you might go bananas, try to book a date night for the two of you, where no wed-chat is allowed, or write a short and sweet note to whoever is driving you potty and ask them to ease up. Just be sure to keep the endgame – a long and happy marriage – in sight.

you're
invited

How to start planning your wedding

Ping! A few months after my own big day, I received an email from a friend. Subject line: HELP!

It was six months before his wedding day, his work had transferred him to Boston, and despite endless nights of transatlantic wedding-planning Skype chats, he and his fiancée weren't sure what to start organising, or even if they knew everything they had to actually organise.

That's where the *From Yes to I Do* to-do list started its life. It's a checklist of all the various parts of a wedding, so you won't forget a thing. It's the Countdown Planner found at the back of this book on page 253 (Added Extras B). Try not to get freaked out by its length – not every element on the list will apply to you, and in any case, like some monster work assignment, it can just be useful to break the planning down into stages.

It begins with one decision you can't escape making, whether you're planning on tying the knot while snorkelling in the Caribbean or in a big white dress in front of your nearest and dearest in a local hotel, and that's *when* you're going to get married.

Picking a date

As a first decision goes, this can be a tough one. What are your priorities – a long engagement, a particular location, meeting your budget, or all of those things? Picking the season is a good place to start working it out: do you want to get hitched in winter or summer? Spring or autumn? Some brides and grooms will want a long engagement, and others want to sprint down the aisle. Be warned, too, that some venues are only open during certain months of the year, and also that the date you choose could have a big impact on costs: traditionally, winter weddings are cheaper because they're less popular, so suppliers drop rates. However, that's not always true – the romantic winter wedding where weather is less of a concern means demand has evened out.

Most venues will offer last-minute discounts for those booking a date, say, two or three months away. You may also be more likely to secure your top venues, favourite photographer, etc. in winter than spring/summer, when their dates may book up more quickly.

A little heads-up, though, that summer dos can lead to a psychological problem known as ATTWF – or addiction to the weather forecast. In the lead-up to the big day, it's easy to confuse 'weather forecast' with 'wedding forecast' – you visit your venue, spot the blooming rose garden and gorgeous gardens and become desperate to celebrate outside. But a spot of rain won't make or break your day, and if you think about it, very few days of the year see solid rainfall all day, so try not to stress – you'll probably still be able to get outside for some photos, at least.

Adrian Stone, an experienced videographer, has a warning though: 'The last great summer we had was five years ago, and since then it has been nothing but rain, mist and fog. The UK has one of the most unpredictable weather patterns in the world – I am still amazed when

I see brides and their family get upset when their beautifully planned summer wedding is washed out.

'If your heart is set on a hot summer wedding with blue skies and gorgeous weather, get married in the south of France or South Africa – countries where, when the weatherman forecasts seven days of hot sun, he actually means it.'

But Adrian is South African, so he might be a bit biased! To make a 'when to wed, weather-wise' decision based on facts, the Met Office has a useful page telling you average rainfall, sunshine and temperature during all the months of the year at tinyurl.com/metofficemaps. And since you can never guarantee sunshine – or a dry day – in Britain, if your heart is set on an outdoor ceremony, be prepared to have white wellies on under the dress . . . Or an indoors Plan B just in case!

Beyond time of year, think about what is the best day of the week for your wedding too. Yes, Saturdays are traditional, but you could save money (and skilfully eliminate any people you don't actually want to be at your wedding but *have* to invite) by going for a midweek wedding date.

Whatever you opt for, it's a good idea to book your ceremony and reception venue – if there are two – at the same time. Booking one, only to discover the other is full up that day, will be a hassle, and possibly expensive too if you end up losing the deposit.

After picking a date, some brides and grooms like to send out 'save the date' cards to ensure everyone they want to be there is free. Be careful, though: it's tricky to uninvite someone if you later realise your venue is too small/your budget is stretched/you actually can't stand them – so only send these to people you're sure you want to invite. Or you could just phone or email key people ahead of time and let everyone else wait for the invites.

❝ I wish I'd thought of that ...

Tom married Elizabeth in May 2012 in Lezant, Cornwall.

'Like many couples we were really, really, I mean REALLY, worried about the weather. The wedding reception was to be held in a barn at Lizzie's dad's farm. Fine, one would think ... it's May after all! We became obsessed with the long-range weather forecasts for the day, which were convincing us it was going to pour with rain. It was our constant talking point.

In the end, three days before our wedding, baking temperatures moved in and we were lucky enough to get married on a cloudless day. You really can't worry about what you can't control! Try and find the little things about the day that your friends and family will recognize as unique to you and your partner.' ❞

Choosing a location

Where you wed will depend entirely on the kind of ceremony and party you want. With religion less of a part of many brides' and grooms' lives and families moving around the country more, nearly-weds are often opting for exotic, exciting and often faraway locations, rather than choosing their childhood church and a nearby venue. A survey carried out by YouGov found that the average British couple shells out more than £1,500 each year on attending weddings – that's all the expense of parties, presents, outfits, accommodation and travel.

If you're a family-minded couple who just want to be surrounded by your closest friends and relatives, it's probably a good idea to marry in a geographically convenient place – somewhere that the most possible important people will be able to get to. For most of us, that sadly rules out St Lucia.

If you are keen on getting married abroad, there's good budget news: you can often organise package deals for nuptials overseas, depending on where you pick, which can work out cheaper. But you'll have to be OK with the fact that you'll likely have far fewer guests, and accept the fact that some important people, like older relatives or those with big families and/or busy jobs, may not be able to attend.

In the UK there are thousands of wedding venue options, depending on whether you're getting married with a registrar, and so need a licensed site, or opting for a church or other religious ceremony and just need anywhere with room for dinner and a boogie afterwards. The venues chapter (Chapter 2) lists sites where you can search for locations for both the ceremony and reception according to your top priorities, be they a late licence to party or a big enough venue to hold the world and his (new) wife that you want to invite.

HOME-MADE DETAILS

One way to say thanks to your guests for taking the time to attend your special day is by making it personal to them, and you, with home-made details like favours, a cake table for dessert or DIY invites. You'll find ideas dotted throughout the following chapters which you can personalise to your tastes. To lessen the stress, try to start on these details as early as possible so you can plan and work slowly. Another way to ease the workload is to encourage friends to get on board too – it'll be more fun in a group, and they will (hopefully!) love feeling a part of your big day.

Paying for it all … the budget

One of the scariest things about weddings – more terrifying even than the first dance – is paying for it. Brides are supposed to walk down the aisle with something borrowed, but none of us want that thing to be cash. Yet the average wedding in Britain now costs more than £20,000. To put that into perspective, it costs something like £2,800 an hour for the average 3.30pm-till-midnight wedding. You could probably get Beyoncé to do a personal performance (for, oooh . . . about 12 seconds) for that rate.

One of the most toe-curlingly horrible elements of the wedding day industry is the firms that exploit brides' and grooms' dreams of a celebrity-style day and offer extortionate 'wedding loans' which they claim are available to even those with bad credit ratings.

But often the interest rates are so steep that the debt will probably still be around on your tenth wedding anniversary, or even on your twenty-fifth. Starting your lives together in debt because of a big white wedding day sadly makes your chances of marital success much lower: financial worries are one of the biggest reasons for couples divorcing.

There's no better reason than that for avoiding any spending on your big day that will necessitate going into the red. The only really important thing about a wedding is the marriage at the end of it and the really wonderful things any guest remembers about a big day are the cheap-as-chips ideas, like amazing vows or personalised messages. If you are totally obsessed with having a massive party that you can't currently afford, consider postponing for a year and embarking on some intensive saving and working overtime; otherwise, stay sensible, make a budget that's affordable, and stick to it.

There are lots of free online wedding-budget planners that will help you work out what to spend on what. But first, the awkward bit: you need to know how much you have to spend. So if you think your parents, other relatives or anyone else may be financially helping you and your partner out with the wedding costs, you're going to have to have A Conversation about it. It's never going to be easy to talk about money, especially if it's with your gonna-be in-laws, but sit down with them over a drink or a meal, ideally with the engagement excitement still fresh (hey, it might encourage more generosity).

If anyone seems embarrassed or vague, explain that you want to be sensible (there's no point planning visits to Westminster Cathedral if your budget is going to be more suited to Warrington Register Office or, indeed, vice versa), so you need to work out what you can spend in different areas. People may want to contribute a set amount, or they may instead prefer to be responsible for a particular part of the day (flowers, transport, catering, etc.), or perhaps they are unable to contribute at all. Whatever the outcome, it's best to know early on. Oh – and a wild-card idea that wouldn't suit most people but is worth having a gander at: one bride and groom got their entire wedding sponsored to secure all

How much will it cost?

In 2013, 21% of weddings in the UK cost under £5,000

36% cost £5,000 to £10,000

35% cost £10,000 to £20,000

7% cost £20,000 to £40,000

Just under 1% cost more than £40,000

(Excluding honeymoon. Source: Confetti.co.uk)

their suppliers without paying a penny. Apparently it's common in America, where some brides even, um, walk down the aisle with a sponsor's logo on their dress . . . Strange but true: check out mybigfatsponsoredwedding. com for a UK bride's version.

Once you do know of any sums people are able to give towards your wedding day fund, pulling together a guest list (not a definitive list of who's coming and who is going to sit where – that joy is still to come – but a rough guide to give the gist of numbers) will help you to establish what your budget needs to be.

When that's done – take a deep breath – it's budget time. My (now) husband loves a bit of Excel, and wedding-related spreadsheets were pretty much his only contribution to wedding day planning, but the extra guidance available from budget-makers on specialist sites such as Google weddings (google. com/weddings/plan.html) and My Wedding Dreams (myweddingdreams.co.uk/budgetplanner.php) make spreadsheets simple and these templates help you think of most details (Google's is particularly exhaustive).

Some rough quotes from suppliers (newly-wed friends may be able to supply estimates) will help you to put numbers into your spreadsheet. Generally, the average wedding bill is made up as follows:

WEDDING BILL CAKE CHART

- VENUE (PLUS CATERING)
- FLOWERS, ENTERTAINMENT, TRAVEL
- CEREMONY
- PHOTOGRAPHY / VIDEO
- DRESS
- HONEYMOON

Try to add a financial buffer zone – unforeseen costs always pop up, such as tips and dress-alteration costs, so when you've got your final figure, add about 5–10 per cent extra for contingencies. If that number dwarfs your total spending budget, see if you can prioritise rather than go into debt.

A bride with 10,000 Facebook snaps who is never seen without a camera will probably see a pro photographer as a must-have, whereas a shy bride who is wary about the idea of a lens being nearby all day might just want pro photos at the ceremony so she can stop stressing about it at the party, so costs can be cut that way. Music buffs might want to book an amazing band, while just-get-up-and-dance cheesy music-lovers could be happy with either a DJ or an iPod playlist stuffed full of their favourite tunes.

A bride I know whose best mate was a chef asked him if he would bake a wedding cake as his gift. He offered to do a dessert buffet too, which freed up some of her squeezed budget for another element of the day. When planning, try to organise your budget so wedding day must-haves are at the top, and go from there to balance your books. The less-important parts nearer the bottom of the list might have to be cut back – but don't despair because it's just as likely that you'll be able to find a home-made or cheaper alternative.

'While planning my wedding I was blown away by ideas in wedding mags and started dreaming of having both a photo booth and vintage ice-cream van on site,' says one bride-to-be who wed near the beach in Cornwall. 'But once I realised each would cost something like £1,000, I sternly reminded myself that neither guests slobbering over Mr Whippys nor friends grinning like goons in passport pictures were vital parts of a happy wedding day, or a successful marriage. Friends set up a camera on a tripod inside an MDF home-made box and in front of a white sheet, with a box of excessively stupid fancy dress gear nearby, and made us our own fab (and cheap) DIY photo booth.'

Before thinking about increasing your budget so it matches your wish list and going into debt, try to be imaginative, ask friends and family for help (financial and/or practical – people love to help and feel part of a wedding) and spend carefully. To help you save towards your big day, consider putting aside a set proportion of your salary into a regular saver bank account (find the best-paying rate at moneyfacts.co.uk) as a wedding fund. Be clever with what you're saving too: one couple who worked in a supermarket last year saved up 40,000 Nectar points over 18 months, and used them to cater their entire wedding reception – with quiches, sarnies and sausage rolls on the menu.

Put your wedding budget in perspective...

Michael Douglas and Catherine Zeta-Jones (2005) – £1m

Tom Cruise and Katie Holmes (2006) – £1.4m

Elizabeth Hurley and Arun Nayar (2007) – £1.7m

Paul McCartney and Heather Mills (2002) – £2.4m

Elizabeth Taylor and Larry Fortensky (1991) – £2.6m

Chelsea Clinton and Marc Mezvinsky (2010) – £3.3

Wayne Rooney and Coleen McLoughlin (2008) – £5.25m

Kim Kardashian and Kris Humphries (2011) – £6.5m

Petra Ecclestone and James Stunt (2011) – £12m

Prince William and Kate Middleton (2011) – £22m

Vanisha Mittal and Amit Bhatia (2005) – £43m

Prince Charles and Lady Diana (1981) – £72m

All figures are for total wedding expenditure and adjusted for inflation

10 easy money-saving ideas

Could you...?

1 Go off-peak. It could be a midweek wedding or just opting for a morning ceremony and afternoon tea, but booking your big day in an 'off-peak' slot could help you make big savings on your venue costs, and give you much more haggling potential with every other wedding day supplier. Think of it like this: if they know they'll either be twiddling their thumbs at home on that Thursday evening, or catering/shooting/hosting your big day, they're likely to go lower for you.

2 Cut your guest list. The more people you invite, the more invites there are to buy, meals to arrange, drinks to organise, and it could even mean having to pay for a larger venue. This problem is often made easier by idea number one: only the people who really love you and want to celebrate your big day will take a day off work for you! If you need to cut down further on numbers, consider making the day adults-only. Be wary: any parents told to leave their offspring at home generally won't be offended if it's a blanket ban, but if you include some kids and not others, you could trigger an upset on the day. Lastly, if you or your fiancé(e) have a really big family and you just don't have much spare room, you might need to explain to friends (and/or distant family) that you're limited on numbers and are having to make a rule on couples – such as spouses and live-ins only. If you can't fit everyone in, or not everyone can come, it's worth looking to see if your venue is online and can hook up 'wedcasting' – using Skype to screen the nuptials from afar – which is especially great for anyone abroad or elderly and unable to make it to your venue. Cutting down on the number of 'VIPs'– like having fewer bridesmaids, ushers, flower girls,

10 easy money-saving ideas

etc. – will also help you to trim spending on extras like bouquets, buttonholes and cravats.

3 Recruit friends. Whether it's your amazing-at-baking aunt making the wedding cake or artistic best friend doing the table plan or flowers, if someone near and dear has a creative talent, ask them if they'll help you out – it could even be their wedding gift to you. Or get a group together for a task like invite-making or putting together the order of service, with your best-handwriting friend doing the calligraphy, and call it a party.

4 Pick a clever location. If you, your fiancé(e) and most of your friends and family all live in one place, this might not work, but more often than not a chunk of the guests will come from Aberdeen and another load from Cornwall. So if that's the case, and a lot of people are going to be travelling anyway, opt for somewhere nearer the less-expensive location – usually outside of main cities.

5 Think about the timing of the day. A 3 p.m. ceremony, for example, might mean you have to serve guests canapés, dinner, plus a late-night snack, depending on how long the festivities go on for, but if you kick off at 5 p.m., you'll only need to shell out for canapés and dinner.

6 Consider all-inclusive. Opting for a hotel or restaurant package that offers the reception, wedding breakfast, booze and entertainment all in one often works out cheaper than organising each individually. Then if you want to make your day more personal, you can spend more time and money on tailoring with DIY details such as photos, table decorations, personalised table names and more (see pages 184–6 and 193–216).

10 easy money-saving ideas

7 Ditch the invite. Yes, it's non-traditional, but setting up your own wedding website and emailing out the link means you can be much more imaginative with your love story, share more plans with your guests, and really make a splash. Not convinced it can ever be as wow-inspiring as a paper invite? Check out jessandruss.us/ – what happens when an illustrator and a web designer get together: so good it went viral. Alternatively, if you still want paper invites, set up a website with an RSVP form, directions to the venue and gift-list details to save having to have extra inserts and pricier stamps in the invite.

8 Borrow something. Alongside something blue, new and old, it's a crucial part of the recipe for wedding preps anyway, so why not make it something like a borrowed venue (would a family friend's garden play host to an amazing dinner?), vintage dress (you've always admired that picture of your grandma on her wedding day – is the dress still lingering in your mum's loft?) or a friend's posh car to pick up the bride?

9 Be a trendsetter. Yeah, you could pick the pricey band that all your friends have booked for their big days, and hire a caterer to whizz up plates of beef Wellington for everyone, but if you start scouting out gig nights to find some new kids on the block that get everyone dancing, or opt for catered food from your favourite local restaurant, you might give jaded wedding guests a happy surprise as well as cutting your bill.

10 Cut the cake. No, seriously, cut it out. It's one of the biggest wedding tax offenders. If you like the ritual of cake-cutting, get a small, posh cake-for-two made for the photo opportunity, then serve guests either a plain cake, cut up behind the scenes, or just dessert.

The practical business of marriage in the UK

Before you can take this man or woman to be your lawful wedded spouse, drum roll please for some basic stipulations…

The two of you must be:

- A man and woman aged at least 16 (and have parental consent if under 18 in England, Northern Ireland and Wales) to get married, or a same-sex couple to register a civil partnership.
- 'Free to marry', i.e. you are both single, widowed or divorced, or were in a civil partnership which has been dissolved.

The ceremony will take place at ...

Well, it depends. Not just on your choice of venue, although we'll get on to that in a second, but on your type of service: civil or religious.

A civil service is a legally approved marriage ceremony with no religious parts. These ceremonies can take place in any register office, or at any venue licensed to hold weddings (including thousands of hotels, stately homes, civic halls, etc.). Booking a register office is usually the cheapest and quickest option, but you'll need to organise a second venue for any celebrations that you want to throw after the service. Alternatively, opting for a venue which has a wedding licence means you can host both parts of your big day in the same place if you want to – but you'll usually have to pay the registrar an extra fee for them to leave their office.

The civil ceremony fees also depend on your location. At the time of writing, for example, a register office in Manchester was charging:

- £49 for a basic mid-week ceremony for bride, groom and just two witnesses in its smallest wedding suite
- £100 for a wedding in one of its bigger wedding suite venues, for up to 70 guests on a Monday, Tuesday or Thursday
- £130 for that same 70-person room on a Friday or Saturday.

Or, for those opting to book that Manchester register office's registrars to officiate at a do in an outside licensed venue, fees were:

- £272 for a daytime, midweek ceremony
- £378 for the same on a Friday, Saturday, Sunday or Bank Holiday.

By contrast the fees at a register office in north London ranged from:

- £100 for a midweek wedding in the register office's own civic suite, to
- £350 for a larger room at the register office on a Saturday.

The north London register office was charging nearly-weds who wanted their ceremony to take place in a separate licensed venue:

- £400 for a midweek ceremony
- £450 for a Saturday
- £1000 for Bank Holidays or a Sunday before a Bank Holiday.

The civil ceremony

Contact your local register office to find out their fees. (You can get their phone number via the offices of your local council.) For a civil wedding you'll need to give notice of marriage to your local register office, whether or not you intend to marry in that area, and book a registrar with them. You can give notice of marriage up to a year ahead of the wedding day (and it's a good idea to get it out of the way early, if possible, so it's one less thing to worry about at the last minute. You must do it at least 15 days before your wedding date – and some register offices have really long waiting lists).

Once you've made an appointment to give notice of your marriage, you'll be asked to make an appointment to attend the register office together with your fiancé(e), bringing along proof of identity and address, plus other documents if either you or your partner has been married or formed a civil partnership before. When you book, ask exactly what you should bring with you, to avoid having to go through the rigmarole twice.

You and your partner must have lived in England or Wales for nine days before registering. If all goes to plan, and after paying a fee of £36 per person, the registrar will issue a Certificate of Marriage, usually after about a fortnight, and you may marry in any register office or local-authority-approved premises in any district. At the ceremony, you'll need at least two people there to act as witnesses and sign your marriage register.

There are thousands of venues licensed for civil weddings (see page 38), but be aware that there are some restrictions. In England, Northern Ireland and Wales you usually can't wed outdoors, say in a public garden, impermanent marquee or on the beach, as the law requires a fixed address. Some licensed venues, however, can organise an outdoor wedding if they have a large, fixed structure in their grounds, so if you're keen on this (and prepared to spend months with your fingers crossed for good weather), check with potential venues. In Scotland, it's usually possible to marry inside and out.

The basic civil marriage ceremony takes about 10 to 15 minutes. The registrar gives a short statement about marriage, but the content of some of the ceremony can be tailored to what the bride and groom want. You're not allowed to use religious words in the civil ceremony, but as long as you steer clear of these, you can include readings, songs or music. My advice is to check your choices with the registrar first, though, because you might be surprised at songs that you've been singing in the shower for years that the officials regard as having

Did you know?

In South Korea, the groom has to endure a foot beating before the end of his wedding. Ushers remove the groom's shoes and socks, use a rope or sash to tie his feet together and take turns beating the soles of his feet with a stick – or a fish. Usually a cod, apparently. It's supposed to test the groom's strength.

religious content. Each partner is required to repeat a standard set of promises – these can't be changed, but can be added to – and, if desired, rings are exchanged.

The religious ceremony

What you need to do before a religious wedding depends on – surprise, surprise – your religion. It's a good idea to speak to your religious officiant well ahead of your planned date to discuss any admin or preparation you need to do ahead of time. In general, for a Church of England wedding either bride or groom must have an association with the local parish, but this has become more flexible so it's worth talking to a vicar if in doubt. Instead of going to the register office to post your intention of marriage before the ceremony, in Church of England weddings, banns (formal announcements of the proposed marriage) can be read in the parish church of each of the partners and in the church where it has been agreed the marriage can take place on three Sundays before the ceremony. (Find out more at yourchurchwedding.org.)

For weddings in other Christian denominations, or other faiths, you may need a registrar present to provide a marriage certificate, so ask your officiant, or contact your local register office (as above) to find out. The registrar will know if the venue in which you want to wed is registered; if not, you can have a religious ceremony there but will also need to have a separate civil ceremony for the marriage to be valid under UK law – hence the need for a registrar. If the building is registered, an authorised person has to be at the ceremony to register the marriage and give the couple a marriage certificate.

Church of England and Wales ministers can register a marriage at the same time as performing the religious ceremony, while religious leaders of other Christian denominations, and of other religions, can be authorised to register marriages too but must have a certificate or licence to do so from the local register office. Unless your ceremony will be their first 'gig', your officiant will usually know the protocol, or will know someone who does, so ask them what steps you need to take to organise your ceremony. If the person performing your marriage ceremony is not authorised, you'll have to either book a registrar to attend the religious ceremony, or have separate religious and civic ceremonies.

The standard order of a religious, Christian service is for the groom to wait at the altar, then the bride to enter to a processional tune. Her entrance is usually followed by an introduction from the service leader, then a hymn, reading (often given by a family member or close friend), the marriage ceremony, followed by another reading and/or hymn, the exchange of rings, signing of the register, then recessional music as the bride and groom exit.

Marriage abroad

Most overseas marriages that fulfil the above UK requirements about age and being 'free to marry' are recognised by UK law, but you should contact a lawyer in the UK and the local authorities abroad to check. The Foreign Office website has oodles of info on how to do it. The site will direct you to the British Embassy of the country where you want to wed, if it has one. (The Foreign Office points out that small islands like the Maldives don't yet have an embassy. But if they're thinking of getting one, can I be first to pitch for that diplomatic posting…?) Contact a lawyer in the UK and the local authorities abroad to find out what documents you'll need to get married overseas: for example, couples set to wed in France may need a Certificate of Custom Law from the local Mairie.

Getting married abroad isn't easy: you'll face admin and bureaucracy that may be particularly tough if you don't speak the language or don't have much spare time to visit the country beforehand. Some couples choose to have a small civil wedding in the UK, then a blessing or reception abroad for that reason. Alternatively, your overseas hotel or wedding venue may have a planner who can help you out. If they don't, you may want to seek out and invest in a wedding planner based in that country to ensure that you tick all the boxes to allow the ceremony to go ahead legally. For a step-by-step guide to the admin needed for an Italian wedding, see page 249 (Added extras A).

Did you know?

Dowries

The greatest marriage bonanza ever is thought to be that from Catherine of Braganza upon her marriage to Charles II. The Portuguese were so desperate to secure a marriage alliance with the English that the dowry included the cities of Tangier – giving England control of the Mediterranean – and Bombay.

You might think the dowry exists as much as the dodo today, but not so. Dowries were banned by law in India in 1961 but this was never seriously enforced and in recent years the number of Indian brides being accused of not bringing adequate nuptials payments has been on the rise. In 2010, 8,391 dowry death cases were reported across India.

Meanwhile, in China a big dowry has become a way for the wealthy to show off their riches. The father of Jinijiang resident Wu Yanrong last year gave her husband four boxes of gold jewellery, share certificates in his tile company worth £10 million, £2 million bank deposits, keys to several villas, a shop, and a new Porsche tied up in a red ribbon. It is thought to be the largest modern dowry ever paid . . . for now!

❝ I wish I'd thought of that …

Ellie married James in September 2012, in Dordogne, France.

'As it was to be held in France we knew that we had to be 100 per cent prepared for our wedding before we left Britain. Popping out to the local shopping centre in rural France isn't easy. Still, we managed to forget helium for the balloons, so we had to send an usher to get some on the day of the wedding. Language problems meant he managed to bring back canisters of air! I advise anyone planning a wedding to make lists... And make lists of lists (I've since learned that the Excel spreadsheet of things to do that I'd sent my then fiancé was pointless …).'

The wedding will be at . . .

Venues, budgeting, transport

It's the place you pull into in that white-ribboned car, the backdrop to your wedding photos, the setting that will give your guests the first clue as to the nature of your big day – and there's an enormous amount of choice of venues out there to pick from. So, how to start?

Well, the first factor to consider is *how* you're getting married. If you're having a combined civil ceremony and party in one place then you can only wed in a licensed venue. But if you are having a religious do, or opting for a register office, and are moving on to a party elsewhere afterwards, there is no such restriction. For a list of all the licensed venues where you can host a civil ceremony and celebrations in the same place in England and Wales – searchable by area – visit tinyurl. com/wedvenues. Most local council websites host a list of licensed venues for civil weddings in their areas on their own websites too.

For religious weddings, the ceremony itself may take place in a church, Meeting House (if one or both partners are Quakers), synagogue or other private place (if both are Jewish), or another religious building, provided that the person marrying the couple is also a licensed registrar.

In Scotland there are fewer restrictions. Religious ceremonies can be held anywhere, while a civil marriage can take place either in a register office or at any other approved location in the registration district. You can find a list here: tinyurl.com/scotwedvenues.

In some specific circumstances, people can get married in venues where they might otherwise not be allowed to – for example, if one partner is seriously ill a marriage can take place in the hospital; if one has serious disabilities or difficulties going out they can wed at home, and if one is a prisoner, weddings can in some cases take place in jail.

So once you've worked out the practicalities of whether to have combined or separate venues for ceremony and reception, and where geographically you want to wed, the next decision comes down to personal preference. Want to wed in a castle? Barn? Stately home? Zoo? Sporting location? Restaurant? Woodland? Theatre? You can search through thousands of options – hunting by location or by type of venue – at venue search engines including weddingvenues.com, www.hitched.co.uk/wedding-venues, and tinyurl.com/moreweddingvenues.

Where couples say 'I do'?

40% of British weddings take place in a church or place of worship

23% are hosted in hotels

16% are in historic houses or castles

3% are on the beach

2% are in marquees

16% take place elsewhere.

Source: Confetti.co.uk

It's great that the range of options for wedding venues is now so huge. Anywhere that hosts private events – from local pubs and eateries to art galleries and bars and clubs – can be an option, but you're not alone if you're finding the choices a little overwhelming.

So, how to narrow it down? You can't beat personal recommendations, so ask friends and family about any 'wow' venues they've attended for weddings, and don't forget to ask other potential suppliers, such as photographers, florists, caterers, etc., that you're talking to about suggestions for venues that they've been impressed with, or that fulfil your wish list: these experts go to hundreds of weddings every year so they may have some suggestions you won't come across while doing online or magazine research.

If you and your partner or someone in one of your families has a special place – maybe where you got engaged, your parents were wed, etc. – it could be worth considering as a venue. Alternatively, might a friend or relative have a large enough house or garden and be willing to host your do? If so, it could mean greater flexibility: your pet pooch/horse/goat etc. could be a part of your day, if that floats your boat – and the average wedding-hosting hotel is unlikely to allow this – and there could be many more options for decorating the space to reflect your personal taste.

Don't assume it'll be cheaper than a more traditional venue, though. There are pros and cons of having a 'ready-made' venue like a hotel or restaurant compared to a stripped-bare one like a local hall or house, or a piece of land for a marquee (see below).

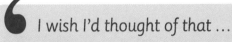

I wish I'd thought of that …

Fiona married Chris in September 2012 at the Hampshire church near where they grew up and they had their reception in hired teepees in the grounds of Overton Rugby Club.

'We built a 10 per cent contingency fund into our budget – it's so easy to go over and you don't want that stress close to your big day. We put any bonuses from work straight into the wedding fund, saved strictly and didn't dip into it – we used a savings account that you can't access straight away.'

Marquees

It's often thought that setting up a tent in a family or friend's back garden is an ideal route to a wedding venue bargain, but, alas, sadly that's not often the case. Opting for a marquee or teepee (not one of those old Native American houses but a tent with one sloping, open side that keeps out the rain but retains the outside view) can actually be pricier. Marquees expert Duncan Russell explains: 'If you want to plan a wedding at home or in the grounds of an idyllic venue or perhaps a simple pasture next to the Thames, you're creating, often from scratch, a unique entertainment space that is only ever going to be used in that way once – so it's often a misconception that it is cheaper to have a wedding reception in a field. If you are on a tight budget then it will often be more cost effective in a permanent venue, but the beauty of having a tented structure is that you get to make everything yours.'

One way to help justify the cost is to max out the space. 'I always recommend trying to use the tents over a couple of events, such as having an informal barbecue for guests who have travelled from afar the next day,' Duncan adds. But then again, all those extra events may cost more too. Having a marquee erected in private land belonging to a friend or family does, though, make it easier to go DIY with the décor – where a hotel banqueting suite might well be in use until a few hours before your big day, here you'll be able to put everything up at least the day before. Self-catering may be more of an option too if a large, available kitchen is on site.

Remember to factor in the extras: you might need to rent loos, power generators, lighting, awnings – and these are not things to scrimp on. 'If you are having anything complicated in terms of electrical supply and distribution then having someone on site from the moment the caterers arrive until the band or DJ start playing to solve any issues with the power is probably the most critical element of a party,' Duncan warns. 'Cold food, in the dark, listening to a personal stereo is no one's idea of a good night...' With that unwanted image in mind, it's a good idea to think about your priorities here – money-saving marquee strategies tend to involve eliminating rain covers and that generator the bloke who deals with marquees said could come in useful. But thinking realistically, that may not be a good idea! So if you're keen on the marquee route, but need to save cash, it may be better to spend less on other areas and keep the piece of material that's going to allow guests to go to the loo without being poured on.

Which leads us to another thing to think about: the weather. Ask marquee suppliers about heating and/or cooling guests – as well as what material their tents are made out of. 'The Great British outdoors is not always favourable when it comes to rain or shine,' Duncan says, 'so if you are having a marquee-style wedding then you should always plan for it to be raining cats and dogs but hope for it to be like the Riviera.' A top tip is to work out a rain plan: for example, if the kitchen and bathroom (or portaloo) aren't right next to the marquee, you might want to think about hiring a covered walkway in case of rain.

> ### ❛ I wish I'd thought of that …
>
> *Duncan Russell has a few tips you should read before signing a hire contract:*
>
> 'Read the booking paperwork and check every detail . . . While as a supplier we always try to make sure everything is captured correctly in discussions on the telephone and over email, the reason that we create the booking paperwork is to ensure there is no miscommunication. With smaller items such as the style of chairs this is not a show-stopper, but imagine a detail like the month or year being misunderstood – it could lead to the equipment being booked out for a different day, causing chaos unless caught at a very early stage.' ❜

Did you know?

Celebrities who wed or renewed vows at Las Vegas' infamous Little White Chapel

Sinead O'Connor

Sylvester Stallone

James Caan

Sarah Michelle Gellar

Britney Spears

Paul Newman

Judy Garland

Joan Collins

Michael Jordan

Bruce Willis & Demi Moore

Frank Sinatra & Mia Farrow

If you're planning on pitching the tent in a field or garden that's missing out on things like parking or accessibility to public transport, think about how guests will get there. And don't forget to have a word with the neighbours too; the simplest way to prevent any moans is to invite them, but otherwise check that they're OK with a day of disruption.

Venue budgeting

The venues that work out cheapest are usually those offering either a lot – such as an entire wedding package – or a little, say renting only a function room or local hall.

All-inclusive deals

These are often available from hotels and generally offer three-course wedding breakfast packages including the drinks, venue hire, cake and DJ for a set fee. That fee obviously depends on the location, level of luxury and inclusions of the venue, but there are plenty of really good deals out there – usually starting from £1,000 – and you'll know exactly what the cost is in advance so you won't have to worry about any surprise costs of music/catering, etc. If you want to get wed soon, the prices drop even more. Hotels and other venues geared up for weddings don't want their function suites to stand empty, making them no money whatsoever, so they will often drop their rates significantly for free days within the next few months, or for off-peak periods. Some even offer cut-price party rates if you can promise to fill up the bedrooms with your guests.

As an example, at the time of writing, a country house in Warwickshire, Woodside, was offering a three-course meal and drinks package for up to 40 guests, canapés at a drinks reception and an evening

Suspicious package?

For hotels and restaurants, weddings are big business, and they will want to squeeze their costs and maximise the profits they make from your big day. Here are three ways to stop them doing just that:

1   Break down the cost of the package they're offering you. Maybe a three-course meal for 100 people, including booze and a canapé-filled reception for £8,000 is a fantastic deal. But if that 'inclusive of alcohol' offer is only house wine, and limited to a stingy number of bottles, or the per-head meal costs soar if you go above 100 people, it might not be. Try to work out the comparable cost of each part of a package you're being offered.

2   Barter — but only on valuable things. If the venue is quiet around your date, they'll likely drop the cost or add extras if you ask. But don't get duped: boosting the number of canapés from five to ten per head isn't going to cost them much extra or wildly transform your day, while hiring a DJ might well do.

3   Know exactly what you're getting. When you visit a venue, they'll usually have set up their prettiest room layout, with fancy chair covers, a big dance floor, etc. But that might not be what's included in the standard wedding package. So make sure everything you see is included, and if any extras are agreed, ask for confirmation in writing.

reception for 70 guests with an evening buffet for £4,000 for bookings between November 2013 and March 2014. This deal also included chair covers and your choice of a coloured sash for up to 40 guests, room hire for a civil ceremony and private use of its bar, conservatory and restaurant all day, a bridal suite on your wedding night plus another two complimentary double rooms for more guests, a supper snack served at 11.30 p.m. of bacon rolls or a vegetarian alternative for evening guests, an MC, services of a wedding planner, DJ until 1 a.m., menu-tasting session, licensed bar until 2 a.m., free use of the gym, swimming pool and sauna for the bride and groom for the three months prior to your wedding day, and a one-night stay with breakfast on your first anniversary (sundialweddings.com/woodside).

Dry hire venues

By contrast, opting to hire a village hall or other site-only booking can be a very different, inexpensive way of securing a wedding venue – and it'll usually be exclusively yours too, which is something that large hotels or restaurants may be unlikely to offer you. It also means you can do as much – or as little – of preparing for your big day as you want, including transforming the décor, organising your own catering for a buffet and bringing in your own alcohol for a bar, all of which can slash the cost of the average big day. But there are

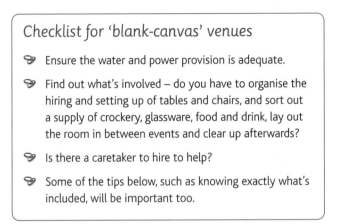

Checklist for 'blank-canvas' venues

- Ensure the water and power provision is adequate.

- Find out what's involved – do you have to organise the hiring and setting up of tables and chairs, and sort out a supply of crockery, glassware, food and drink, lay out the room in between events and clear up afterwards?

- Is there a caretaker to hire to help?

- Some of the tips below, such as knowing exactly what's included, will be important too.

downsides, too: it will involve a huge amount of work and organisation – or outsourcing to willing friends and family!

Visiting a venue

You can check out every aspect of a venue's website, Facebook page, Twitter messages and friends' photos of previous weddings there, but really, there's nothing to beat visiting a venue to help you work out if it's the place where you want to wed. Try to organise visits so both you and your partner and, if possible, parents or other friends or family members can come too. More heads might be able to spot any flaws or plus-points at particular sites – although you probably won't want

❝ I wish I'd thought of that ...

Rachel married Troy in June 2012, in the gardens of a relative's house in Buckinghamshire.

'I had to hire everything from a generator upwards, and deal with a lot of different companies to put together a wedding for 140 people in, basically, an open space. It took a lot of time and organisation, and I'd only recommend doing it this way if you genuinely love planning big events. We had loads of friends and family come the day before and help decorate, which was really fun and a great part of the weekend. The only thing that I'd have changed is that I would have had heating in the marquee, as June 2012 wasn't warm.' **❞**

to bring too many people to avoid being bamboozled by opinions. It's a good idea to write down questions in advance, based on your priorities for the day. These might include those shown in the box opposite.

It's a good idea to pop a camera and a notepad in your bag when you go to visit a venue, to jot down details and to help you remember the rooms and areas that you're shown around (they can quickly all merge into one . . .). When looking around, especially if it's made up for a wedding, don't let yourself be wowed by the decorations. Think of practical stuff too, like are the

Venue checklist

🍃 What's the capacity – for the ceremony and/or reception and/or sit-down dinner?

🍃 Is there a minimum guest count?

🍃 Is there an outside option – if it's not raining – for a drinks reception/kids to run around/fireworks at the end of the night, etc?

🍃 Is there parking?

🍃 Are there any noise restrictions?

🍃 How many events do you host per day? (This is particularly important in larger venues if you don't want to run into bride number two – or three, or four – on your big day.)

🍃 Is there an on-site wedding planner?

🍃 Can I bring in whichever caterer/florist/cake, etc., I want, or do you allow in-house or selected suppliers only?

🍃 If I bring in my own caterer, are there kitchen facilities for them to use or would they need to bring in these too?

🍃 What's the total venue cost? What does that include, what extras could be incurred, and when are payments due?

🍃 Are tableware, cloths and glassware, etc., included?

🍃 If we opt for an in-house supplier, what are the catering costs and what's included?

Venue checklist

🍃 What other extras do couples sometimes opt to pay for?

🍃 How many tables fit in the wedding breakfast room? At full capacity, how large is the dance floor? Is the size changeable?

🍃 Are you licensed to provide alcohol?

🍃 Can we bring in our own alcohol?

🍃 Is there enough sound, power and lighting built into the venue or do we have to bring our own or ask suppliers to do so?

🍃 Is the venue disabled-friendly? If so, does this cover all parts of the venue including toilets, and all rooms?

🍃 Are we allowed to do our own decorations? Are there any restrictions on what's allowed on the walls? Are candles OK? And confetti? Professional firework displays? Chinese lanterns?

🍃 If it's a hotel, do you offer cheaper deals for guests who want to stay over?

🍃 How long does it usually take staff to turn a ceremony room into a space for a sit-down meal or reception?

🍃 Is there a set time at which the celebrations have to finish?

🍃 What is the cancellation policy?

🍃 How much time will I (or my suppliers) have to arrange the room in advance of the big day?

loos nice and are there enough of them? Is someone on hand to check them during the party? Think about if it rained – can you access all areas indoors or under cover? Is there enough parking and how long would it take to travel to the venue from the places from which most of your guests will be departing? Is it near a train or coach station? Is there a good room, or area, for photographs? If you're having two separate venues for the ceremony and party, think about how easy it will be for your guests to get from A to B, and whether both venues will hold the same number of guests easily – you don't want your party to look lost in one venue or be squashed into another.

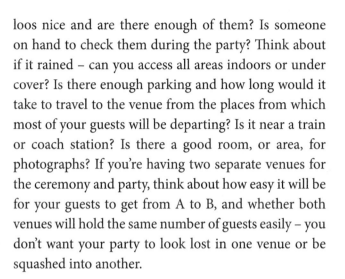

Did you know?

The German wedding reception tradition of 'kidnapping the bride' sees the best man whisk away the bride to a local pub, where they hide out until the groom finds them. When he does, he must pay for all they drank.

Paying for it

It's not exactly as fun as trying on wedding dresses, but reading through every word of a venue's contract to make sure you're happy with it is really important.

One tiny mistake, like a wrong number making the timing or date incorrect, may be difficult to fix later on. If you can, ask an events or legal expert to help you read through all the terms and conditions.

The contract should include the total cost and detail of exactly what's included for that price (rooms, tables, chairs, wedding planner, etc.), the payment terms for the deposit, when and how the balance is due, the date, time and location(s) of every part of the wedding, contact details of the person coordinating your day, and the cancellation policy. It's a good idea to check that any other details you have requested and the venue has agreed to offer are listed in the document too – don't assume the wedding planner nodding when you ask if you can have candles makes it OK. Also, check when it is that the date is reserved for you – it could be on signature of the contract, but it may be only after a deposit is paid.

Most venues will demand a deposit, usually paid in chunks at defined periods before the event, as well as payment of the full hire cost a few weeks before your big day. With marquees, it is usual for suppliers to ask for half the fee six months beforehand, and the remaining payment around three weeks before the event.

'For an event that is 6–12 months away an appropriate deposit is in the region of 50 per cent and you need to really question the reason behind any supplier asking for 100 per cent for something that is happening next year,' marquee expert Duncan advises. 'If your own cash flow is tight then do ask your suppliers if they are able to stage the deposit payment over a number of months. We often get asked this and, dependent on circumstance, it's a way we can help our clients as they make their plans.'

Budget option?

If the budget won't stretch, hotel chain Premier Inn offers a £199 deal – including bride and groom's outfits, a buffet reception for up to 20 guests, the wedding cake, confetti, best man's speech template, a two-night honeymoon at a Premier Inn – and pyjamas (but they do come from Primark).

Get me to the church/temple/synagogue/ venue on tiiiiiiiiime

Whether you fancy jumping out of a plane in your wedding regalia or pulling up in an old Mini, hiring out a horse-drawn glass carriage à la Jordan or surprising your guests by turning up in an ice-cream van, tuk tuk, riding pillion on a Vespa, hailing a London taxi, or squeezing into the rust bucket that you and your other half drove around Europe together when you got engaged – remember, anything's possible! Well, maybe apart from the plane; it might eat into the rest of your budget, be a bit rough on bridal wedding hair, and possibly reveal more of a wedding-day garter than anticipated.

Anyway, like the other elements of the wedding, how important you think your wedding transportation will be to your big day will influence how much you want to spend on it. Your venue will also have an impact. Many brides who get ready at their venue didn't bother hiring a special car, either foregoing the tradition altogether or decorating the family car with a thick white ribbon (found at simplyribbons.com but also available from local haberdasheries, or stores like Hobbycraft).

Sprucing up a car you have, or borrowing a fun or flash one from a friend or relative, can be an easy way to slash one extra wedding cost. And it's so austerity-chic that even Wills and Kate did it – driving out of Westminster Abbey in Prince Charles' old motor. OK, so his was a vintage convertible Aston Martin, but it's the idea that counts.

If you've no luck tracking down a cool car to borrow, or you're keen on making a big, unusual entrance or exit, there are a lot of options out there:

Classic car

A vintage ride like a Rolls-Royce, Jaguar or Bentley always looks fab in photos – sleek and sophisticated. Shop around. If you're getting hitched in the countryside, the deals will usually be cheaper than from hire firms in London or other cities. Look for options that let you hire the car by the hour or per job, depending on your needs. If you're travelling to a separate location after your ceremony and will want the car to whisk you and your new husband or wife away at the end of the evening, an all-inclusive day rate could work out cheapest. But if you just need a ride from home to church or venue, and some snaps of you doing so, then an hourly pricing scheme might be cheaper.

A word of experience from a friend who turned a shade of blue during the hour-long drive to her winter wedding in a vintage Bentley: always check whether a vintage car still has vintage heating – as in… none. That's one modernisation you may want to have on board. And a roof in case of rain?

Sports car

The acceleration could be useful if you're running late, and a bright red Maserati Gran Turismo, Ferrari Enzo or Lamborghini Gallardo will bring a splash of colour to photos too. Look at the hiring options as above – often these supercars come with packages lasting a few days, so bride or groom can enjoy the cars a few days before or after the wedding if they want. But watch out: if you're going to be driving the car rather than hiring one with a chauffeur, check you can get insurance and include those (often hefty) costs in your calculations. Getting pulled over by the police isn't a fun just-married experience . . .

The bride might want to practise getting in and out of the car too: not always easy in jeans and a T, let alone a wedding dress, whether it's slinky or meringue. Alternatively, why not hire a stretch limo? They offer a bit more room.

Taxi

A cheap (well, compared with renting a Rolls) route to getting an iconic ride in London is to hire a black cab, either hailed off the street (though you or your other half would need to have cash on board) or booked in advance through firms like londonblacktaxis.net/blog/wedding-taxis or tinyurl.com/wedcabs. Exclusive hiring usually costs from around £70 an hour and vintage cabs are available too.

Relax . . .

Every day in China there are 27,000 weddings. So it can't be that hard . . . right?!

If you're getting hitched abroad, cabs can be an extra-cool and budget-friendly option. A New York cab, say, will be a great reminder in photos in years to come of the city where your wedding took place. In other parts of the UK – or world – the local cab might

Other unusual transport ideas

A colourful VW – or VW camper van

Double-decker bus with the destination board showing the bride and groom's names

Horse and cart

Tractor

Tank

Golf cart

Helicopter

Fire engine

Police car

Harley-Davidson

Milk float

Ferry across the Mersey

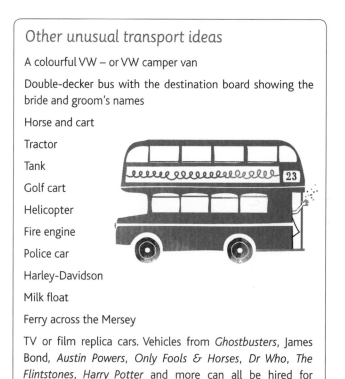

TV or film replica cars. Vehicles from *Ghostbusters*, James Bond, *Austin Powers*, *Only Fools & Horses*, *Dr Who*, *The Flintstones*, *Harry Potter* and more can all be hired for wedding days – see suppliers such as starcarhire.co.uk.

not be quite so instantly recognisable or chic, but local firms sometimes have a special Jaguar, Mercedes or BMW in their fleets and may agree to reserve it for you for an afternoon for a cheaper price than a traditional wedding hire car.

Top tips for embracing ethical and going green

🪱 **Ethically sourced rings** – Jewellers in the UK aren't allowed to sell bling from conflict zones. But smuggling and dodgy dealers makes it difficult to find out the origin of some stones. The only way you can be sure you're getting an ethically mined stone is to ask see a conflict-free guarantee. Safer still, you could make your own rings – there are workshops at colleges around Britain, such as londonjewelleryschool.co.uk. Or you do a Prince William and pass on a family rock, or buy vintage and revel in a retro ethical look.

🪱 **Trim the paper trail** – e-invites are one economic and effective route to reducing paper, but for those wanting their invites to arrive via a letterbox rather than an inbox, try recycled paper, an invite made from cotton (artcadia.co.uk), wood (suppliers include woodcard.co.uk) or even a tea towel (weddingteatowels.co.uk)

🪱 **Thought for food** – The wedding breakfast, booze and honeymoon can all come with hefty carbon footprints, but it's not hard to reduce one or all. If you specify you want seasonal produce then most caterers should be able to find suppliers within the UK. A local cider is easy to

Even though it's your wedding day, traffic still builds up, tractors still tootle along country lanes at 5 mph, and rain still slows everything down – so try to build lots of spare time into your journey schedules. Take a dummy ride, work out how long the journey(s)

Top tips for embracing ethical and going green

source and will impress guests – especially in winter when it can be served warmed and spiced. Wine is tricky as English red isn't to everyone's taste, but our white and sparkling wine would pass the Pepsi Max challenge with most continental varieties.

- Flower power – Many traditional wedding flowers are shipped from the other side of the world, making demands on your wallet as well as on the world. You might want instead to try sending out friends, family and bridesmaids on a bonding experience gathering local wild flowers. Or just ask your florist to stay in season and native. You could also use potted plants and herbs as decorations and then offer them to your guests as gifts.

- Watch the air miles – A flightless honeymoon might not tickle your fancy but you can pay a little more and green-wash your guilt by opting to offset your plane's carbon emissions, either through travel agents or flight websites, or via companies like climatecare.org. Alternatively greentraveller.co.uk deals only in stunning destinations you can reach without flying.

will take, check there are no special events (football matches, car boot sales, etc.) that might impact your trip (and find an alternative route if so), and add a wodge of time to avoid being late anyway. You can always take a spin around the corner a few times if you're early, but if you're late it'll just mean more stress, and sweaty moments.

Any huge delays might even mean the ceremony could be postponed – if a registrar has a backlog of ceremonies to officiate at, for example, they might not stick around to wait 30 minutes or more.

Guest transport

If your wedding straddles two venues, or you have a large number of out-of-towners staying in a hotel or nearby without their own cars, you might want to think about organising a mini-van, coach, party bus, or just mini cabs to get your guests from their hotel to the wedding and back again. Likewise, if you're hosting an out-of-town wedding and lots of people are staying over, offering guests transport is one way to guarantee they'll stay till the end and help you to dance the night away. Alternatively, and more reasonably, you could ask guests (especially close friends and family) who are driving if you could fill up their spare seats with out-of-towners and non-drivers.

HOME-MADE DETAILS: GUEST BOOKS

Having a gift list for presents often means you don't receive many wedding cards, so if you'd like the people at your wedding to jot down messages about your big day or their hopes for your lives together, a guest book can be a nice idea. The likes of WHSmith and Paperchase sell these for about £20, or if you want a more unusual or personalised option, the internet is fertile with ideas. These include drawing (or roping in someone artistic to do so) a large, branch-filled tree, and providing ink pads so each guest can make a 'leaf' fingerprint and sign their name (or buy a version at tinyurl.com/weddingtreeprint), asking guests to write messages on the sides of Jenga tiles (meaning you have both a game and a bunch of great memories at the end), or buying a large, inexpensive china plate or platter and providing indelible pens for guests to write memories on something you'll be able to put on the wall of your home. Another cool idea spotted on bridal blogs is setting out an old-fashioned typewriter and stack of paper for guests to write messages. (Typewriters are often sold cheaply at charity shops.) Or you could ask guests to contribute to a wedding 'wish tree' which has been set up with dangling ribbons or beads and luggage tags for guests to write on. There are lots of other ideas at tinyurl.com/marthaguestbooks.

Alongside the guest book, it can be a good idea to prop up a card with some questions such as where guests see you, the bride and groom, in 25 years' time, their funniest memories of you, or their top marriage advice. This means that instead of receiving a guest book full of lots of heartfelt but slightly dull (like a birthday card signed by colleagues!) messages wishing you congratulations, you'll have a book full of probably hilarious and touching ideas.

Decide whether you want your guests to arrive before or after you at the venue. Arrive too long before a slow coach full of guests and you could find yourself having too much time alone in the reception. It is nice to have some downtime though, and it's a good opportunity to get those couples photos taken.

The people and events

Running orders, roles, music and readings

The order of the day

Weddings in this country haven't yet stretched to the US/Hollywood-style almost-a-whole-week-long version and rehearsal dinners are still pretty rare over here too. But you'll still be surprised how many parts there can be to fit into a wedding day, if you want to include them. For a sample timetable for the bride's morning prep, see page 125, where a make-up artist reveals her brides' usual timings to help you work out your own.

As for the overall timings of your day, they will obviously depend on when and where you're kicking off the celebrations. Some grooms have a pub lunch with their ushers before the ceremony, while some brides like to have their bridesmaids and best friends round for champers. Timings will obviously also differ for morning and afternoon ceremonies, and for those having a reception immediately after the ceremony or weddings with a gap in between, where more guests then join you for the wedding 'breakfast' (the confusingly-named meal that sometimes refers to the nuptial lunch or the dinner but never involves Shreddies). However, see pages 67–8 for a rough guide to the various parts and order you may want to build into your big day.

The people

Brides: Who do you want to be around you as you dress on the morning of your wedding and to plan a hen of epic proportions for you in the weeks leading up to the big day?

A rough running order

- **Preparations** – for the bride these are likely to include make-up, hair and dressing; for the groom, general getting ready plus sometimes a meet-up with ushers for a pre-wedding pint or lunch.

- **Photos** – sometimes of the bride and her family and the groom and his family before the ceremony. If time is going to be tight after the ceremony, some couples opt for formal photos before the service.

- **Guests begin arriving** – the role of the ushers is to guide the guests to the right seats/location for the ceremony and give out ceremony leaflets/order of service if provided.

- **Ceremony** – the officiant will run through order of service.

- **Formal photos** – these are usually for close family, plus some bride and groom shots. Ask the best man or an usher/bridesmaid who knows all of the relevant people to group the photo stars in the photo area to save time.

- **Reception** – for everyone else. This usually lasts an hour or 90 minutes if there's a big room turnaround to take place.

- **The meal** – the newly-weds are announced to the room full of guests.

A rough running order

🍬 Speeches – usually a welcome speech from the father of the bride, then a meal, but if other speech-givers are particularly nervous and would prefer to get them 'out of the way', the father of the bride's speech is sometimes followed immediately by the best man's speech and response from the groom (and sometimes the bride too).

🍬 Dinner – sometimes interwoven with bursts of dancing.

🍬 Speeches – this is the usual time for speeches from the best man, followed by the groom.

🍬 Cutting the cake – this is sometimes followed by a photo of all of the couple's friends.

🍬 First dance.

🍬 Dance the night away or other entertainment.

🍬 Carriages – just before the end of the evening, the bride may do her own speech or have another end-event, like fireworks, Chinese lanterns, or even something simple like guests forming an archway for the bride and groom to pass under as they leave.

Grooms: Who is the one bloke (or woman) in your life you'd like to make a speech about you and your wife on the biggest day of your life? Who you can also trust not to handcuff you to a lamppost the night before the wedding bells ring (unless that's your idea of a good night out…!).

Bridesmaid(s) and the best man aren't the only roles that form a part of the average wedding day. Depending on the size and formality of your ceremony, there may also be civil witnesses, religious witnesses, maid of honour, page boy(s), flower girl(s), toast-givers, readers, singers, people to be a part of the aisle procession, ushers, ring bearer(s) and a bride's giver-away-er.

Usually the person doing the latter job and accompanying the bride in *that* walk (or choreographed dance – apparently it's a hot new trend in aisle-walking) is her father. But it doesn't have to be, and you don't have to be given away at all. People think weddings are very set in stone – they're not; most of the key parts of ceremonies you see in films and at other people's big days are traditions, and if you want to follow them, great; if not, make up your own traditions. No church or civil venue requires this role to be filled.

But it is a good idea to think about exactly who you want to be involved in your big day as early as possible. They will need to prepare and this could mean learning a reading off by heart or writing a speech, but equally could involve planning a fake nine-hour kidnapping stag-night session. Even if they don't need to plan anything, you'll want to maximise the chances that they'll be available to make your day, and not on holiday or working, so give the people you want to be involved as much notice as possible.

Having said that, be careful not to ask anyone without thinking hard about the decision first. It's awkward and difficult to *un*request anyone's involvement. There may be financial ramifications too – some brides decide to pay for their bridesmaids' day, including dress, shoes, bouquet and accessories, and even organise a pro to do their hair and make-up too – and if that's something you want to offer the top women in your life, you might not want to have six of them. Likewise, if you're the kind of person who gets flustered and you are worried about being stressed on the morning of your wedding, it might be a good idea to have fewer manic 'maids around, and pick calming people who relax you. You can always give other friends or family alternative roles, such as being a witness on your civil wedding certificate, introducing guests and handing out ceremony leaflets or confetti, or giving a reading during the wedding service.

Perhaps take a few minutes to think about the jobs people will be doing before handing out specific responsibilities. Obviously most men will want their best man to be their best friend or brother, but if said best friend absolutely hates public speaking talk to them about it first, or consider having two best men – one to make the speech and one for other roles, such as organising the stag and looking after the rings.

BEST MAN WANTED!

WANTED: One top chum/relative to arrange an epic stag night, including returning groom to bride in one piece; help groom plan his wedding day outfit, including being honest if suit makes him look like an overweight penguin; smile sweetly when the mother-of-the-groom/bride asks, for the fifteenth time, if his best man's speech will be 'blue'; lead ushers in their duties for the day; keep the groom company at the altar; look after the wedding rings; look after any admin or money needed to be given to suppliers on the day; marshal key family members into the formal photo area (and remember that Great-Granny Ethel needs a chair to sit on); give a witty, sweet speech that makes guests laugh and mothers of the bride and groom swoon; tie tin cans and other amusing things to bride and groom's getaway car; look after the groom's suit or return to hire shop if necessary after the big day . . . Salary? Well, none to speak of, but you can surely get them on board with the opportunity to totally humiliate their best friend/bro/etc. on a stag and take photos that will be worthy blackmail for life.

MAID OF HONOUR/BRIDESMAID(S) WANTED!

WANTED: a sister/BFF to join the bride at dress fittings, agree that the dressmaker is DEFINITELY wrong because said bride's bottom is tiny and the material does not need letting out; organise an epic hen night; sort out the other bridesmaids on the big day and ensure all have their dress, accessories, etc. just right; help the bride prepare on the morning of the big day (including providing a chilled bottle of champers, if desired); walk down the aisle then smooth out the bride's veil and train when she arrives (without stealing the bride's thunder – we're thinking of you, Pippa Middleton!); hold her bouquet if required; look after a stash of spare lipstick, pair of flats, etc. for the bride; bring her water if she looks flushed during dancing; look after her all night long and decorate the newly-weds' room with rose petals, etc. Salary? No cash, but everlasting friendship should cover it.

> **I wish I'd thought of that …**
>
> *Lucy married John in August 2011 at Prestwold Hall in Loughborough.*
>
> 'My advice for newly-weds is to stand your ground and do what you both want – ignore the nagging MILs-to-be, religious obligations and domineering wedding shop assistants. I regretted not having my Scottish Highland bash. Remember, in the long run you aren't going to make everyone happy, and if they can't deal with that, then tough! My other top tip would be never say the word 'wedding' to anyone – they add pounds on immediately. I told a few of my suppliers that I was organising a sixtieth birthday and had everything delivered to the office beforehand, which saved me a lot.'

MC

A master of ceremonies can be an important person in helping weddings – especially big ones – run on time. You might associate an MC with being an old geezer with greased-back hair, bright red coat, lots of gold medallions and really cheesy dad-jokes. In some cases you'd be right, but if there's anything complex about your big day – say, a large venue, or lots of aspects to introduce, or people arriving/departing at different times – these people can really help keep things on schedule and prevent you running out of dancing time at the end of the evening.

If your venue has an on-site planner helping you out on the day, he or she will usually be able to help with behind-the-scenes work, making sure the band or DJ is ready when the meal finishes, etc. Otherwise, it's worth thinking about an MC. 'Time just disappears on a wedding day . . . what would normally feel like an hour on a normal day feels like 25 minutes on your wedding day,' says videographer Adrian Stone. 'There is a lot to fit into the 8–12 hours a normal wedding lasts; you need to ensure things keep moving along. It is very easy to fall a few hours behind if you do not have someone overseeing the schedule.'

Often friends or family are willing to help out. Just make sure they love public speaking, will hold off on the champagne until the evening and are pretty organised. It's a good idea to do all their prep work for them in advance – such as telling them exactly what they need to do and when, giving them a detailed schedule for the night, asking them to keep intros brief – oh, and you should probably buy them a big thank-you present afterwards . . . I'm told it's a stressful role!

Ceremony music

The tunes to which you wed will vary enormously according to the type of wedding service. If you're getting married in your childhood church and have been in the choir for years, you probably already know what you want. If you're a hip-hop fan tying the knot in a register office, you might want to go untraditional.

Ultimately, whatever music you pick for your wedding will be a personal choice. Do you want live music, say an organist, cellist, choir, etc., or do you prefer recorded tracks, sung or played by the original artist? (Note: at civil ceremonies the tracks must all be non-religious.) Usually brides and grooms can have music during various parts of the ceremony, not just when walking down the aisle but also hymns and songs during the service and/or during the signing of the register where it might be a bit quiet otherwise.

There are lots of 'wedding music albums' with classic tracks like Wagner's 'Here Comes the Bride', but you don't have to go down the conventional route. Just check with your service officiants that they are happy with your music choices beforehand – and that their organ/piano/ choir is up to the task of playing your preferred tune.

If you're struggling for inspiration and are thinking of booking a ceremony musician, use their expertise – ask them what tunes they've played at other weddings, or have seen work really well. Alternatively, the Wedding Music Company (weddingmusic.co.uk), a firm which provides musicians, bands and DJs for ceremonies and receptions across the UK, has a website that offers a huge amount of inspiration for both booking music experts and checking out tunes, with easy-to-listen-to snippets and suggestions.

Some popular music choices for . . .

Civil ceremonies

FOR THE ENTRANCE OF THE BRIDE:

'Canon in D' – J. Pachelbel

'The Prince of Denmark's March' – J. Clarke (trumpet and strings)

'Air', from 'The Water Music' – G. F. Handel

'Eternal source of light divine' – G. F. Handel (soprano, trumpet and strings)

'Air on the G String' – J. S. Bach

'Morning Mood' – E. Grieg

SIGNING OF THE REGISTER:

'Dôme épais' – L. Delibes

'Chanson de Matin' – E. Elgar

'Nella fantasia' – E. Morricone

'O mio babbino caro' – G. Puccini

'Largo ma non tanto', from 'Concerto in D minor for Two Violins – J. S. Bach

'Minuet' – L. Boccherini

THE RECESSIONAL (bride and groom exit):

'Wedding March from A Midsummer Night's Dream' – F. Mendelssohn

'Arrival of the Queen of Sheba' – G. F. Handel

Some popular music choices for . . .

'Trumpet Tune in D' – H. Purcell (trumpet and strings)

'Allegro, from Brandenburg Concerto No.3 in G' – J. S. Bach

'Trumpet Voluntary Op.6 No.5' – J. Stanley (trumpet and strings)

'Radetsky March' – J. Strauss

. . . and for religious wedding services:

FOR THE ENTRANCE OF THE BRIDE:

'The Prince of Denmark's March' – J. Clarke

'Wedding March from Lohengrin' – R. Wagner

'If ye love me' – T. Tallis

'Gloria in excelsis Deo' – A. Vivaldi

'Eternal source of light divine' – G. F. Handel

'Trumpet Tune in D' – H. Purcell

SIGNING OF THE REGISTER:

'Ave Maria' – F. Schubert

'Laudate Dominum' – W. A. Mozart

'Jesu, joy of man's desiring' – J. S. Bach

'Ave verum corpus' – W. A. Mozart

'The Lord bless you and keep you' – J. Rutter

'Dôme épais' – L. Delibes

Some popular music choices for . . .

HYMNS:
(With hymns it can be a good idea to print the words in the service booklet – this avoids a whole lot of heads-down muttering and embarrassed looks.)

'Praise, my soul, the King of Heaven'

'Jerusalem'

'Dear Lord and father of mankind'

'Love divine, all loves excelling'

'Glorious things of thee are spoken'

'Guide me, O thou great Redeemer'

RECESSIONAL:

'Toccata from Symphony No. 5' – C. M. Widor

'Hallelujah Chorus' – G. F. Handel

'Wedding March' – F. Mendelssohn

'La Réjouissance' (Music for the Royal Fireworks) – G. F. Handel

'Prelude to Te Deum' – M-A. Charpentier

'Arrival of the Queen of Sheba' – G. F. Handel

Readings

Maybe you're getting married in a church but you haven't been in one for, ooh, the best part of a decade, and feel a little overawed when you learn they want you to pick a bit of the Bible to read out. Or perhaps you're worried about a civil ceremony being a bit bland and want to add a dose of meaningful readings but have no idea where to find them. Don't worry. As in so many wedding-inspiration ways, the web is a lifesaver. These sites host hundreds of suggestions, ranging from the Bible (but civil wedding-ists watch out: your readings cannot be religious) to *Winnie the Pooh*. They may also help inspire you if you're writing your own vows.

Try:

- hitched.co.uk/speeches/readings/readingshome.aspx
- youandyourwedding.co.uk/planning/readings-speeches/readings-and-poems-for-civil-ceremonies/154.html
- toast-masteruk.co.uk/page/wedding_poems_and_readings
- itakeyou.co.uk/wedding-ideas/wedding-readings-poems.htm
- guardian.co.uk/books/2011/apr/23/wedding-carol-ann-duffy-poetry

The speeches

Oh, the speeches. As a guest at someone else's wedding, these often seem to go on. And on. Until you're wondering if it would be rude to scrape back your chair and tiptoe round the edge of the room to escape to the bar. Or anywhere where Best Man Bob's toe-curling ramblings about Groom Gary's ex-girlfriends aren't going to be audible.

You might not think so, but speeches average around 40 minutes in the vast majority of weddings, according to Adrian Stone, who says: 'Everyone seems amazed when I tell them this, but it's true and so it's important to plan and schedule accordingly.'

So when organising a wedding breakfast's timetable (your caterer and/or band should be able to help with this), some people find it useful to give each speech a time slot: 10 minutes for Dad, 10 minutes for the best man and 20 minutes for the groom is the norm. Even if you give each speaker a maximum amount of time, it's best to build a few extra minutes into the schedule for them to run over (apart from anything else, getting to the mic and pausing for applause takes time), which will mean you're more likely to be able to stick to the schedule and not have to curtail dancing time at the end.

'For those weddings where the speeches can go on a lot longer, you do need to be careful,' Adrian adds.

'Unless someone is a stand-up comedian or a brilliant public speaker they can become incredibly boring. Make sure everyone has timed their speech – the worst I have seen was a dad's speech going on for half an hour when it should have finished after 10 minutes. Choose your best man carefully too. Unless he is really funny, tell him to stay away from the jokes – and make sure he doesn't mention anything too risqué. Mentioning the groom's porn collection as the greatest in the world is not something you want the in-laws to hear or, worse yet, the bride, if this is news to her . . . and when he goes on and describes it in detail, it really is time to get him away from the mic . . . .'

Having said that, it's probably not a good idea to write a 15-page dossier of 'speech suggestions' for the best man – it could backfire and end up being mentioned in his speech . . . . But if you want certain people to be flagged up for thanks, or mentioned in memory, bring it up ahead of time. If the bride's father doesn't mention *that* person you wanted him to, or the best man doesn't bring up that anecdote you really wanted everyone to hear, you can't blame them for not second-guessing you.

As for the actual speech's content, how to write that is an issue so debated-over that a whole industry has sprung up with writers scribing other people's wedding speeches on their behalf – for a fee, of course. It's not easy, and as you sit in front of a blank laptop screen or empty notebook with major difficulties working out where to start, that paid-for option might sound appealing. But a from-the-heart personal speech – even if it has the odd stumble or shaking hand during delivery – will always be nicer than a slick professional job full of standard clichés.

Entertaining kids

If you've got a lot of kids coming to your big day and want to keep them occupied, you might want to think about making them activity bags. You can pop some of their favourite puzzles or games in bags (eBay even sells 'thank you for being our bridesmaid/page boy' drawstring bags for £3 or you could easily make your own if you wanted). Pound shops are an easy source of goodies, and by combining a colouring set, disposable camera and a notebook/scrapbook with captions such as 'the bride and groom', 'the cake', 'the kiss', they can capture the day and make a keepsake book. You can buy ready-made scrapbooks or other ideas at tinyurl.com/confettikids, including wedding activity place mats for kids that only cost 85p. Alternatively, if you're really worried about kids going mad and have a lot of them coming to your big day, there are wedding day crèches and other entertainment from suppliers like artfullsplodgers.com and alittlesomethingextra.com. Be warned, though: they're not cheap. As a rough guide, one supplier quoted £270 for a two-hour daytime crèche for up to 15 children, plus £100 for each additional hour.

Speech therapy

Some tips if you're struggling to work on a speech:

1   Jot down a list of things you want to say. No need for funny or clever phrasing (yet) or a genius opening line: just write down the simple things you want to say, such as people to thank or mention, memories or stories to tell, and any presents/props to bring along/refer to. Grooms, you'll have the most to pack in. You'll probably want/need to mention the bride and her dress (and how wonderful she looks!), and to thank both sets of parents, the ushers, best man, bridesmaids, organisers and the guests for coming. It's a good idea to talk to the bride about anything she wants you to fit into your speech too – especially if she isn't doing her own – and ask her for ideas on things to mention. I did this with my husband, providing ideas about things to mention about my parents and siblings, for example.

2   Don't stress too much about how to start; 'Ladies and gentlemen' works well for a formal do, or grooms might want to kick off with 'My wife and I . . .' – everyone is bound to cheer or clap – whereas clichés like 'They say this is the best day of your life, so is it all downhill from here then?' sound boring and impersonal.

3   Do actually write words down. Just because you once delivered a genius drunken rant/speech in the pub, or have an amazing Oscar acceptance speech you devised off pat in the shower, this isn't a good time to rely on memory. Write down your speech either in full or in note form – even if you know it off by heart. Nerves do

Speech therapy

funny things, and you don't want to forget anything (or, more importantly, anyone).

4   Remember everyone is on your side. It's a wedding, not an awards ceremony: the people in the room with you *want* your speech to be sweet, funny, loving – all the things you do – and they're going to laugh and clap as long as you give them a tiny opportunity to do so – like mentioning the bride looks amazing or that her mum has done an incredible job helping to organise everything or even just by holding up the bride or groom's bedraggled 20-year-old teddy bear.

5   Funny is good; sentimental is great; rude is not. Remember there are likely to be grandparents and stiff-backed aunts in the room. Don't swear, or bring up *that thing* that happened on a friend's stag night five years ago . . . Keep it pre-watershed!

6   Don't go on. Keep to the time allowance you've been given in the schedule. Short and great is better than long and dull.

7   But take your time on delivery. Don't race through like the terms and conditions announcer at the end of an advert. Relax, take a deep breath at the start, leave pauses for guests to absorb jokes and stories, and they'll be putty in your hands.

8   Last tip: don't drink too much beforehand. Plenty of time for that afterwards . . .

Dress code

The dress, the suit, the other dresses, accessories

This might be the only time in your life when you get to decide what on what outfit your nearest and dearest will be pulling out of their wardrobe for a day. Most guests like to know roughly what to wear, so a dress code can be helpful. Black tie, for example, tends to add a dash of glamour, lounge suit is sometimes more comfortable for an outdoor summer affair, while if the two of you love dressing up, why the hell not have a masquerade do? Likewise, more casual dos might forego a dress code altogether.

The most common wedding dress codes are one of the following, from the most to least formal:

Morning suit: most weddings see these longer-jacket combos reserved for just the wedding party, if at all, but some people like their extra formality. Since very few guests are likely to own these, though, be aware you might be adding to their expenses with a clothes-hire bill. And that could come off your present!

Black tie: this means tuxedo time for men. The real McCoy involves a dinner jacket, dress shirt and dress trousers, while some go for a cummerbund too. For women, long glam dresses are the norm, although shorter but still wow dresses are pretty common too.

Lounge suit: it's a normal suit and tie job for men, and usually a shorter-length dress for the ladies.

Casual or wear what you like: some brides and grooms want a more low-key affair or prefer everyone to be comfortable all day long and so keep the dress code casual. This might be more appropriate for your do – activity weddings, for example, like picnic dos might be tricky to negotiate in a ball gown. But expect to get a lot of phone calls from your guests asking what to wear if you put something vague like 'wear whatever makes you happy'.

Now, on to another type of dress code entirely . . .

The dress

Has ever an outfit had more invested in it? You want to look a billion dollars; you want to take his breath away, but you don't want to shock Great Aunt Martha into an early grave, and you still want to look like yourself – just a better version of yourself.

Maybe you've already tried loads of dresses on; maybe you're still getting over the fact that some bridal boutiques charge (as much as £50) for appointments and will only refund this if you buy a dress. Talk about pressure!

But try to have fun with the process – and don't worry if you don't fall in love with a dress in the first shop you visit. Start your search by booking appointments at a few bridal shops. It's a good idea to be upfront about your budget, but be wary: the assistants are salespeople, and may usher you towards dresses that cost more. Lots of bridal shops will proffer you champagne so it can be fun to take along a trusted relative or friend (although maybe not a whole gang of them, otherwise you can end up getting more opinions than an average UN session every time you try a dress on, and end up confused and frustrated.

That's true, too, of how many dresses you look at, according to dress designer Sassi Holford. 'When you start looking for your dress, less is definitely more – only make appointments with the designers whose dresses reflect your personality,' she says. 'During each appointment do not try on too many dresses. Buying a wedding dress is a unique experience and you cannot treat it like buying any other dress. You get a tingle when you try on your first wedding dress and if you try on 48, anything after the fourth is just not going to give you that feeling and you'll start viewing them as disappointing and stop seeing the dresses in perspective.'

Your first bridal boutique trips could just guide you towards working out exactly what kind of dress you want, or could see you leave with an actual dress on order. You might think the prices are fine or even have a family member willing to buy it for you, or you might just use the designer costs as a source of inspiration for a less expensive dress elsewhere. Either way, everyone's experiences are different so try not to feel worried if you don't fall in love with a gown straight away.

'It took me (and my very patient and excited mum) ages to find my dream dress,' one summer bride says. 'I'm small – short, skinny, etc. – but not Polly Pocket small. So I was kind of surprised when I went into bridal shops and they pushed half a sofa cushion down the back of a dress to make it stay up. Other shops asked me to stand on a small table when a dress was way too long. The first time this happened, I was really admiring the dress, thought it might be The One, until I realised what I actually liked was how tall I looked. You couldn't see the table under its layers of duchesse satin – and the dress was pretty average.'

Try to bear in mind that even though your gown might be a fairy-tale dress style, it might also have to be a practical choice. For example, if you're getting married on a beach in Sri Lanka, a meringue dress with cathedral-length train won't be easy to pack, or

---

The bill

Wondering how your dress costs measure up?

28% of brides spend up to £500 on their gown

16% of dresses are £500–£750

31% cost up to £1,000

22% are up to £2,000

2% are up to £3,000

And less than 1% cost more than that.

Source: Confetti.co.uk

wear on sand, and might get a bit hot too. If you're getting married somewhere religious, there may be restrictions, such as needing a shoulder covering. Ask your officiant first, though, and assume nothing. I once spoke to a rabbi who said he'd arrived at a wedding to find the bride wearing a shoulderless black mini-skirt dress. He was shocked (mainly by the black colour, he claimed) but still wed the couple that day and they remain happily married!

It's also worth thinking about the likely temperature on your wedding day when considering fabric choices. Some dresses can feel like wearing dumb-bell bands at the gym, but all over the body, and might seem tough to sport for 10 minutes let alone 11 hours. Likewise, don't feel you have to wear white. This 'traditional' colour was first made popular by Queen Victoria in the nineteenth century, as the colour worn by debutantes when they came out into society, but in Eastern cultures, brides often choose red to represent auspiciousness. You could opt for a totally different colour entirely. Certainly, for those of us with pale skin tones that make snowmen look tanned, a traditional 'white' dress can make us seem to 'disappear'. Ivory is often more flattering for pale skin tones, while a brilliant white dress looks great on redheads and darker-skinned brides.

When it comes to the actual style of dress, your own shape and taste should be the biggest influence.

But from years of working with brides at her Chelsea boutique, Sassi's advice for choosing the right shape of dress for a bride's figure are:

- **Full bust:** You can balance a bigger bust by wearing an A-line or ballgown skirt shape to create a perfect hourglass.
- **Small bust:** Try a sweetheart neckline, plunge or halterneck style to create more curves.
- **Petite:** If you have a small frame, steer clear of very heavy fabrics or bulky designs that will swamp you. Try an empire line as this will work to lengthen you visually.
- **Wide hips:** If this is you, avoid horizontal seams across the widest part of the hip, as they will only add more width.

Rest assured that the thousands of dress designs out there, from strapless to lace overlay, meringue to straight and slinky, short-skirted to long-trained, mean you'll definitely find one to suit you. So don't stress about it, and enjoy the search.

Cutting dress costs

If you love a dress but find it is way beyond your price range, don't despair. Designer dresses can easily cost tens of thousands of pounds, but no one's going to be peeking inside your dress to look at the label. Desperate

> ## Trying-on tips
>
> As every good (ex) Brownie knows, you should always be prepared. If you want to wear a veil, try one on with the dress; if you're going to wear heels, take a pair with you to your fitting – it's hard enough to totter around in a dress that feels very different from the jeans you probably wore in to the shop without adding a pair of shop-borrowed shoes that don't fit. And if you're planning an up-do for your hair, it's a good idea to twist your hair into a bun so you can have an idea of the overall look.

for a particular dress by a famous name? Look out for sample sales where you could find your dress for a fraction of its list price – you can find information about events like this near you in bridal magazines or free online at sites like bridesmagazine.co.uk/events. Be aware, though, that in wed world, sample gowns tend to be sizes 10 or 12.

The same is true of gowns on sale at wedding shows – one of the biggest is the National Wedding Show: nationalweddingshow.co.uk, and it has racks of fairly inexpensive wedding dresses. Trying one on in a makeshift changing room in an exhibition centre may not be the romantic experience you had in mind, but there is always a huge range of designs, sold at a discount because 'what you see is what you get'.

Another idea is to find the dress you love second-hand. Unlike other definitions of second-hand, a wedding dress really is likely to have only been worn once, for less than 12 hours, then dry-cleaned. You can find them on sites such as stillwhite.co.uk, bride2bride. co.uk, preloved.co.uk and sellmyweddingdress.co.uk, which sell designer dresses from bridal brands such as Brown's Brides, Caroline Castigliano, Pronovias and Vera Wang, in as wide a range of sizes as they are on sale when new.

Also online, eBay sells thousands of bridal dresses, but here, as on all websites, make sure you're happy with the honesty of the seller, and ask for lots of photos plus, if possible, even a copy of the original purchase receipt

I wish I'd thought of that ...

Nickie Gott is Managing Director of wedding planning group She's Gott It!

'Underwear is a big one that people tend to forget when packing and getting ready at the hotel or venue. Although I must say this is generally the groom not the bride! Also, organising things like who walks Mum down the aisle. When planning, always have a to-do list and cross things off as you go. Start at the finished event – look, feel, content and design – and work backwards.'

to ensure the dress isn't a copy of a designer dress. If a dress is on sale at a price far cheaper than all the rest, be wary and ask for evidence of its provenance.

Some shops also host 'designer days' where the dress designer is in their store, will sketch you any alterations or add-on ideas, and may offer deals. While these don't usually lead to brides wangling a discount on a dress, they may see you given a free veil or shoes. Alternatively, department stores like Debenhams, John Lewis or House of Fraser, plus discount store TK Maxx, also offer off-the-peg dresses; most cost around £500, but brides report snapping them up for a steal in the sales.

If you opt for a bespoke design by a dressmaker, seek out recommendations, look at his or her other designs and/or speak to previous clients to ensure they were happy with past work. It's a good idea to think about whether you like the dressmaker too – getting a dress made can involve weekly fittings and you might find yourself seeing your dressmaker more than some of your closest friends. For that reason, it's also a good idea to find a dressmaker who isn't too far away from your home or work.

Or you could do the total opposite and find one thousands of miles away. This is a wild-card idea and you'll have to have plenty of time, but China's wedding dress industry is booming, and eBay is filled with happy reviews from brides who have ordered made-to-measure wedding dresses on the site. This isn't a purchase where you want to just click 'buy' – instead, do your research: ensure the seller has a top rating, and ask lots of questions about sizing, delivery and design. Request fabric samples, check reviews, and get in contact with past brides to ask how they found the experiences with particular sellers/tailors. When totting up the cost, don't forget to factor in extras such as postage (which can be as much as £75) plus VAT and customs duty of around 30 per cent of the agreed fee.

You can also find inexpensive wedding dresses – and, if you excuse the Miss World-sounding sentence, help the world – at charity shops. Barnardo's, Red Cross and Oxfam are among the charities which have specialist bridal shops – see tinyurl.com/barnardosbride, visit tinyurl.com/redcrossbride and tinyurl.com/oxfambridal, where all of the dresses available in stores are also listed online. Some of the dresses are even brand-new donations by designers.

Again, when calculating the final bill, remember that a sample dress or second-hand gown may also involve a delivery fee, and perhaps another round of dry-cleaning if it would make you feel happier. Be wary, this is expensive! Wedding dress cleaning can cost more than £100. You may also need to factor in alteration costs, in case the dress doesn't fit perfectly.

❛ I wish I'd thought of that . . .

Dafna married Jilpesh on Easter Saturday in 2010 near Bradford.

'I got my beautiful dress from a charity shop (and nobody could tell – £70, what a bargain!) and bridesmaids' dresses in the January sales. We only had a photographer at the church and just after, so two hours at most. He charged £250 and gave us a CD of all the photos, meaning we made our own album. We then put blank CDs on all the tables with our address on for guests to take home to put their photos on to and send to us. Our album from Bob Books cost £70 so we saved a fortune that way, and having everyone's photos arrive in the post was really fun.'

It's also worth asking family if there are any amazing bridal gowns lingering in someone's loft – my cousin wore her mum's wedding dress, altered by a really talented seamstress so it looked like it was made for her body, and it looked wonderful. You're guaranteed to set older family members reminiscing about the dress, and you could help start a family tradition. If a dress isn't quite right or hasn't weathered the years well, take it to an alterations expert to see if it's possible to give it the Cinderella treatment.

Wherever you decide to source your dress, once you have found one that you love, stop! Don't try on any more – you'll drive yourself mad. Congratulate yourself on a job well done, arrange your fittings, and switch your shopping to focus on shoes, underwear, or any of the other things on your to-do list.

If you surf a few wedding photographers' websites, you'll notice some brides are actually wearing two dresses – a long, elaborate one for ceremony and photos, and another more practical one for partying. 'It's a growing trend,' says dress designer Sassi – who, surprisingly, says it's really unnecessary. You can have the best of both worlds with a clever dress design, such as a long train that clips on top of your dress but can be removed for the dancing part of the day, or a bustle to hoik up some of your train. 'Eye-catching accessories can transform gowns through the wedding day,' Sassi adds. 'A beautiful dress and a long-sleeved jacket are perfect for the ceremony, for example, but then for the more relaxed evening party, the jacket can be taken off to reveal a strapless décolleté gown, the veil or tiara swapped for clips or even a few flowers. Add some more glamorous jewellery and maybe lower heels for dancing and you will still look suitably bridal but with effortless glamour.'

For older brides, fashion guru Jan Shure offers advice. 'If you want the whole nine yards of tulle, you have an entire bridal industry out there to help you find it. Some older brides want something that will make you feel gorgeous, glamorous and special, but not the same gown you might have worn if you were marrying at, say, 25 or 35.

'Your choice will depend on the style of celebration – a register office demands something chic, like a dress and coat or dress and jacket, or even that endangered species a skirt suit; for a hotel-style celebration you may want something more glam and 'red carpet'. If the nuptials are on a beach somewhere warm, you will want something long and flowing yet still appropriately grown-up.

'The good news is that choosing a gorgeous dress in a cut that suits your body shape and in a colour that truly flatters you, and then styling it cleverly, is a much better guarantee of fabulousness than how much you spend. And you certainly don't have to choose white, but you may want to choose a colour at the paler end of the spectrum. Shades like oyster, nude, shell pink, peach, palest grey, eau de nil and cream are flattering and will look bridal but elegant and grown-up.'

Accessories

If you can, pick out your wedding shoes as early as possible, because then, whether you're getting a dress made or having an existing one altered to fit, you can ensure the length is perfect. You'll also have more time to wear in the shoes, prancing around the house in them to make sure they don't start pinching on the one evening you definitely want to dance the night away. Some brides opt to squirrel away some pumps, bridal trainers or even embroidered Converse (check out these beauties: tinyurl.com/conversewedshoes) to switch into later if they are not comfy in heels.

At the other of the scale, a lot of brides like to splurge on Jimmy Choos or Manolos for their wedding – if that's what you want, go for it, but you might want to go for a re-wearable style in that case: ivory isn't all that useful for other dates in your diary.

Brides who are struggling to find comfortable shoes to go with their dress: you're not alone. I spent months looking for this Holy Grail, and eventually discovered sites online where you can design your own shoes, such as upperstreet.com and shoesofprey.com. Upper Street also has a studio where brides can visit before ordering their wedding shoes, at no extra cost, and can design personalised shoes that fit perfectly and match your colour scheme (you can go for a purple heel and contrasting upper, for example). Bespoke shoes are pricey, around £300–£400, but if you're considering spending that on a designer shoe, at least this way your pair will be unique, be inscribed with your wedding date if you so wish, and actually fit.

Extras like a veil, tiara and garter are great things to use as your 'something borrowed', otherwise there are bargains galore online: sites like weddingveilsdirect. co.uk have options in every size and colour, plus a veil-buying guide to help you work out the length and shape of veil you want, from short 'blusher' (cheek or chin-length) right down to super-long waterfall veils, including multi-layer, and those that include beads or crystals.

Watch out for really long ones, though. 'The dear veil, in my experience, is the greatest source of pissed-off brides,' videographer Adrian laughs. 'I can appreciate long veils – they look elegant and timeless and add that special something to your ensemble. The challenge, however, that no one seems to mention to the unsuspecting bride, is that the two men closest to her, her dad and husband-to-be, are going to be standing on that long, beautiful veil multiple times, as you arrive and leave the church, yanking at your carefully prepared coiffure.

'I have lost count of the number of times I have seen brides get seriously irate with their dad, and then their husband on their wedding day, all because of the veil. So do still have one, but adjust your expectations

I wish I'd thought of that …

Anna married Saul in March 2011 at a hotel in the West End of London.

'Everyone had said to me that the day would go really quickly so I was expecting that but I didn't expect it to finish before I'd said hello to everyone. I wish we had thought beforehand about the people we wanted to make sure we spoke to at the wedding.

And remember, it is just one day and you shouldn't lose sight that this is a marriage. There is no point having arguments with your in-laws over the colour of the tablecloths or the font on the invitation; you will be spending the rest of your lives with these people so don't fall out over something petty before you've even begun. Also, for every conversation you have about your wedding with your fiancé, make sure you have one about your marriage. Have the discussions about where you want to live, how many children you want to have, how religious you want to be, etc. While this might seem a little serious, it helps to keep the bigger picture in view and it's really exciting to plan your future together.'

accordingly and prepare yourself emotionally and mentally, that when the two men closest to you step on it you won't go bananas. You could try warning them not to, but . . .' Dads, grooms, brides: you have been warned.

The day after the wedding, it's a good idea to ask your mum, maid of honour, bridesmaid or someone else you trust to take your dress to the dry cleaner to get it returned to its former glory, if you're heading off on honeymoon immediately. Most firms will box the dress up under special tinted plastic to stop it discolouring in the years to come.

The groom

The main man in the wedding party is often left behind in the search for that ideal wedding outfit. Some may disagree, but it seems to me that there are just not as many sartorial directions in which you can travel with a suit as with a wedding dress. Although there's always the non-conventional options: kilt, 40s kit, getting hitched while dressed as a Smurf . . . I'm sure it's happened on *Don't Tell the Bride* before.

Anyway, where to start the search? If it's a suit, black tie, top hat 'n 'tails or kilt you're after, have a gander at that stack of *Bride, You and Your Weddings* and other glossy mags that your fiancée's friends probably plied her with when you got engaged. Yes, they're mainly full of models in dresses, but you'll definitely spot some grooms among the ladies. Local wedding mags – the type you'll pick up at wedding fairs (or, as they're often called for absolutely no reason, 'fayres') and while trooping round venues – will usually feature the clothes that are on the racks of local stores, so these are a good source of inspiration if you started your groom-kitting-out mission a little later than you should have, or just want to opt for the easy life. Wedding blogs (see index) also host thousands of real-life weddings so you can see what other grooms are wearing, and whether you fancy replicating any of their outfits.

If the big day's dress code is smart, the usual options include morning suit (long jacket with waistcoat), Highland dress (kilt, sporran, waistcoat), military uniform, lounge suit or black tie. Some grooms, however, opt to ramp up their smartness beyond that of the rest of the guests, with groom and groomsmen alone in morning suits, for example. For more time-consuming outfits, like bespoke suits, you'll need to plan ahead, usually ordering at least three months before the big day.

Then there's the 'rent versus buy' issue. Obviously, the former is much cheaper – hiring a three-piece suit will cost an average of £70, while the final bill for buying a suit will depend on the quality, designer, etc, but will usually be several hundred pounds, and even more for dinner suits and tailcoats. But if you're a regular suit-wearer, that option could work out to be better value in the long run, plus you're likely to be able to get a better fit if you buy a suit and have it altered for your body, or a perfect fit by going bespoke and getting a suit made for you.

'Over the last few years we've seen an increase in the number of grooms wanting to buy an off-the-peg suit, or invest in a bespoke suit as a souvenir of their special day, rather than hire,' says suit expert Dave Shaw. 'Made-to-measure suits in particular have become more affordable and are becoming more prevalent.' That's more relevant to those with a lounge suit dress code though: 'With changes of everyday dress codes for gentlemen over the past 100 years, few people possess their own morning suit, so many choose to hire it for their weddings.' As well as traditional tailors and department stores, a growing option for cheaper made-to-measure suits is online: sites such as asuitthatfits.com tell men how to measure themselves, before entering the details online and having a bespoke suit made overseas at lower cost than British rivals.

By contrast, if you're renting a suit, make sure you know about all the costs involved, such as cleaning or insurance fees, and if you're going away on honeymoon immediately after your wedding, ask a (trustworthy!) friend or relative to return the suit to the store to avoid fines. For those getting hitched abroad, some suppliers will offer extended rental deals for that very purpose.

Whether you opt to buy or hire, look out for bulk deals: some suppliers offer the groom's wedding outfit hire for free or at a discount when, for example, three or more wedding outfits for ushers, best man or fathers of the bride/groom are ordered.

Once you've made the buy or hire decision, what about the style? 'When suit hunting, it is important to be aware of your body shape and choose an outfit that is flattering,' adds Dave. 'A well-fitting suit can hide a multitude of sins – even with men who are more portly, or have "grown into themselves" . . .' He says a well-fitting waistcoat can give grooms a 'more streamlined' figure, but it's crucial to ensure that any waistcoat is long enough to cover the top of the waistband. 'Similarly, suit jackets with side vents can be worn by most people, and are particularly good for larger gentlemen as they tend to have a nicer drape,' he adds.

Oh, and don't worry if your best man or one of your ushers towers over you or vice versa: tailoring can help. 'One of the more common questions we get asked concerns grooms and groomsmen of differing heights,' says Dave. 'A common misconception is that shorter men cannot wear tailcoats – but actually they can be better, as the graduated hemline does not give an absolute separation between the top and bottom halves of the body. Similarly, top hats can give additional height as well as a sense of occasion.'

Once the suit is organised, remember to talk about matching colours with your fiancée: if her dress is ivory, say, you may want a shirt in the same colour rather than white, and you might want a tie in the same colour as the bridesmaids' dresses or wedding theme colour. Suggesting a history of scruffy grooms turning up to pick up immaculate suits ahead of their big day, Dave adds: 'Also, ensure that everyone is well groomed: a shave, haircut and clean fingernails will be noted and remembered for evermore!'

❝ I wish I'd thought of that …

Simon married Charlotte in a field in Ireland in September 2012.

'Pretty much everything that could go wrong, did go wrong at our wedding. It began with a blocked sewage pipe, then the marquee couldn't be erected where we'd thought, forcing us to change location with a day to go, it continued when my best man forgot the rings and reached its zenith when the power failed and my ushers had to run around our neighbours' houses trying to warm dishes. Having said that, it was a truly magical and memorable day – and more so for the disasters. My ushers were so good that my wife and I didn't know anything about it until afterwards. My advice: choose your ushers carefully (and remind the best man about the rings!).'

Bridesmaids, flower girls and page boys

Some brides plan their 'maids' outfits down to the denier of their tights, others give them a colour scheme and let them run with it, and many go somewhere in the middle. In general, whatever they wear they will look better happily wearing dresses they like than scowlingly wearing something the bride likes. If you've got bridesmaids who are a mixture of ages and shapes, it can be a lot easier to name a colour and ask them to find something they like in that hue. Otherwise, many brides organise plain cream dresses for kids, and add a sash in the same colour as their older 'maids' gowns.

> ## Colour matching
>
> For those looking to follow or avoid the hit trends, the most popular wedding colour schemes are:
>
> purple, royal blue, navy blue, red, rose pink.
>
> (Source: Confetti.co.uk wedding survey)

If your bridesmaids are footing the bill for their outfits, then they're likely to want to get more than one wear out of the dress, so they might want something less obviously 'bridesmaidy.' Luckily, that's what's in for 'maids at the mo, according to wedding blogger Sonia Collett. 'Don't choose particular bridesmaids' dresses just because they are traditional or expected,' she says. 'It's increasingly popular to have non-bridesmaidy dresses and even mismatching dresses that will suit all your maids.'

For kids, you can find plain cute dresses cheaply at shops like Debenhams, BHS, Marks & Spencer and Monsoon, and even at the supermarkets, such as the Florence and Fred range at Tesco, or online from sites including perfumeriver.co.uk (before making a purchase, join the Perfume River Facebook group to secure a 10 per cent discount).

Ideas for jazzing them up include flowers, ribbons or crystals; check out local haberdasheries and sites such as rucraft.co.uk for inspiration. Flower girls' dresses usually match either the colour of the bride's gown – white, ivory, etc. – or the colour of the adult bridesmaids' dresses, if you're having them. Or two-tone dresses can tie both designs together. If you're getting married in this country, it's a good idea to include cardigans for the kids as part of their outfit – they won't smile for photos if they're cold!

Page-boy outfits are also easily organised – usually either a plain shirt and trousers and wedding-colour tie, or a little suit if that's more up your street. Either way, they're not difficult to find. If you can, try to buy kids' outfits as near to the big day as you can stand, because children have a tendency to grow, especially during the summer holidays when lots of weddings take place.

Grown-up bridesmaids may be trickier. High-street treasure troves – where you can go to one place and find a big range – include Coast (coast-stores.com), who make lots of different dresses in a range of colours, and Karen Millen (karenmillen.com). 'Non-official bridesmaids' dresses from shops like H&M, Whistles, Phase Eight and Zara can work well – they all have a constant supply of pretty and unusual dresses, but may be trickier if your 'maids have different shapes and want different dresses in the same colour, or you want the same dress in a variety of colours for a rainbow effect.

Two other sources of thousands of bridesmaids dresses are Dessy, from the USA, and Two Birds. Dessy (dessy.com) sells 'maids dresses in an astonishing range of colours and designs, making it amazing for that 'one colour, different dresses' idea. Although the make hails from the USA, there are lots of stockists around the UK so you can try the dresses on in stores. Being American does mean the outfits take about 12 weeks to arrive, and though you order the size you want, I've heard of several bridesmaids reporting that the dresses turned out much larger than they were supposed to be, meaning extensive (and expensive) alterations. So if you can, visit a Dessy stockist before ordering (dessy.com/ storefinder) and try for size first. Lots of these dresses are also sold 'nearly new', just like wedding dresses, so scour the bridal re-sale sites listed above, plus eBay, before shelling out.

Alternatively, Two Birds sells one dress which can be worn in about 15 different ways. The dress isn't cheap, at around £200 depending on length preference, but since it's so adaptable – it can be worn as a halterneck, strapless, ruched dress, sleeved, backless, etc. – 'maids might get more use out of it and be happier to spend the money and/or chip in. Its fabric makes it especially useful if one bridesmaid is pregnant (twobirdsbridesmaid.co.uk). For a more unusual look, maidstomeasure.com lets you/your 'maids design their own dresses, either online or over bubbly at its store, for £215–£255.

If you've got time for a group day out on a special dress-seeking visit, designer outlet villages can be great for bargain dresses. The most famous include the McArthur Glen chain (with Karen Millen, Hobbs, Warehouse and Burberry) and the Bicester Village Outlet near Oxford (brands include Donna Karan, Jigsaw and Prada). Online, there are loads of bridesmaid possibilities on Asos – it's got a whole sub-site for bridesmaid and wedding guest options: tinyurl.com/asosbridesmaids.

Mothers of the bride and groom

The mother of the bride or groom is one of the most high-profile people at a wedding after those actually taking the vows, so finding an outfit might feel a bit daunting. 'Only take a friend, husband or family member with you if you totally trust their judgement and don't feel intimidated or bullied by them,' advises Jan Shure. 'We all have that friend/daughter/mum/husband whom we love dearly, but either their taste is a bit iffy, or they put pressure on us to buy something we're not sure about. Sometimes the relationship dynamic is such that you succumb to pressure and buy something you're not totally happy with. If that's the case, it is better to go alone and trust your own judgement, and that of the staff at the store where you are buying.'

Did you know?

A French wedding tradition called the '*Pot de chambre*' sees members of the wedding party making the newly-weds drink from a potty. Traditionally it was filled with a random array of local produce, but nowadays it's usually a new potty filled with champagne or chocolate spread!

Picking a colour is usually one of the first decisions to be made, and to stay on side with your daughter or daughter-in-law-to-be, you may want to ensure it fits in with the rest of the bridal party and the other mum. 'Choose the best colour for you, or if you don't already know which colours suit you and elicit endless compliments, do your own blink test in the shop,' says Jan. 'As you try on something, stand in front of the mirror and close your eyes for the count of 10. As you open them, do you see you or the garment? If it's you, the colour is right; if it's the garment, the colour is overwhelming you and is wrong.

'Try to choose a fit and shape that is right for your body shape. Shop assistants should be able to guide you – they see your shape and proportions and know their stock – but remember, you need to feel happy and comfortable in the outfit. If it is too tight, or too constricting, you won't feel comfortable and that will show. That said, a pair of Spanx can make all the difference to your silhouette. Just don't buy them too small – that flesh has to go somewhere!'

Hat-picking can be tricky for all guests, especially those in the bridal party. If you're wearing one, you may want to know that experts claim a hat should never be wider than your shoulders, and only wear a very small hat if you are very slender and petite. 'If you are wearing a dress and jacket, dress and coat, or a suit, you can wear a stunning hat or structured fascinator, but if you are wearing a long gown, your headwear should be very simple and informal, like an understated fascinator or some gorgeous jewelled clips or combs,' adds Jan. 'And when you are choosing your hat, do remember that you are going to be photographed a lot, so don't choose a brim that hides your face or casts a shadow . . . you want that big smile to be on show in the wedding album.'

Pretty details

Brides often talk about feeling like a celeb on the actual wedding day – and not just because of the flash of cameras on walking down the aisle or the fact that you're the one person in the room that everyone wants to talk to. The prep and pampering on the morning of your big day makes you feel like a VIP – even if Victoria Beckham gets all this done purely for a trip to Waitrose. On my wedding day morning I had my hair done at home (the closest I'll get to being Cheryl Cole), and was practically hand-fed sandwiches by my mum while my make-up artist got to work, then was driven off in a white-ribboned car – all the while being snapped and videoed. Seriously, the preparation part is *really* fun.

Trial runs

Plan ahead and your big day can also be super-relaxing. Wedding make-up artist Paula Kopitko has spent hundreds of wedding-day mornings with brides over the past 20 years. If you're no beauty fiend, don't feel the need to plaster on make-up just because wedding magazines say everyone does, says Paula. 'I believe that on your wedding day you should look radiant and your most beautiful, without anyone saying, "It's the hair or the dress or the make-up," she says.

Some wedding fairs even have a few big stands pushing the idea of getting plastic surgery 'for your big day'. Walk away! You're marrying someone who loves you just as you are – and probably most of all when you're freshly showered and wearing PJs before bed! Much nicer to use the time leading up to your big day to enjoy some relaxing pampering if you like it, and book a make-up artist and hairdresser if you want to and can afford it. But there are plenty of other alternatives.

If you do want to indulge in beauty treatments, Paula recommends brides start doing so three months before the big day. 'It's always good to have a couple of facials before your wedding to allow your skin to look its best – make-up will always sit better if the skin is prepared well,' she says. To track down cheap facial, spa and hairdressing deals, check out Wahanda.com – it's a group-buying site that specialises in beauty treatments. But if you've never had a facial before, don't decide to have one the week before the wedding, or you could break out in spots.

'But,' Paula adds, 'if you need to keep to a tight budget, then instead of pro facials try just stepping up your daily skincare routine. Exfoliate your skin every week to get rid of any flaky uneven skin and boost circulation. Buy a good-quality mask and use it once a week. Don't forget to moisturise – all skins need moisture, even oily skins. Beauty consultants in department stores will be able to offer you lots of advice – and free samples – but don't get sucked into spending a fortune on one brand though.'

If you feel embarrassed about spending time with a particular expert at these concessions stands or you don't actually like what they're doing but feel you have to shell out on the products anyway, there's an easy escape. Just say thank you politely and explain there's a few things you want to buy, so you'll take the product to the till when you're ready to pay for all your purchases. Then if you don't want to buy it, just give it back to another member of staff or place it at a till point afterwards.

Most beauty costs can be trimmed by opting for the DIY route, but if you're planning on having a spray tan before the big day, it's a good idea to call on an expert. Orange marks don't exactly improve the look of a white dress. See if you can trial a tan first (at least four weeks before your big day) and wear white clothes to ensure it doesn't transfer. Paula recommends that 'it's best to have the spray tan done three days before the wedding day so the tan look its most natural, and you don't have to worry about any colour rubbing off onto your dress.'

Oh – and grooms, beauty expert France Baudet advises: 'When trimming facial hair, condition your beard in the shower first. It will make the hair softer and easier to trim with less irritation. Exfoliate to get

Did you know?

Brides and grooms in the islands and some other parts of Scotland still face the tradition of 'blackening' couples before their wedding day. The ritual sees friends and neighbours covering brides and grooms in treacle, soot and flour, symbolically to ward off evil spirits.

rid of dead skin and help prevent in-growing hairs around your beard which surface as red, irritated spots.'

Make-up

If you are looking to book a pro make-up artist for your wedding day, most will need to be booked three to six months in advance. Costs depend on who you're booking, and where you're based (Bobbi Brown herself is going to cost more than Lizzie from the local salon), but a trial will usually cost from £50–£80 and then on-the-day prices can be £100+ for the bride, and between £40 and £60 for other members of the bridal party. 'When looking for a make-up artist always ask friends or family for recommendations,' Paula advises. 'Then when you meet them, ask to see photos of their work. Remember that your make-up has to last 10 to 12 hours and you want to look as good at the end of the evening as you do walking up that aisle.'

Chemistry is important too. 'The make-up artist is the last person to spend time with you before you step into your dress, so you want to be able to feel relaxed, to be able to be honest and say if you want a little more or less make-up, and generally feel calm and unhurried.'

Trials are best done 10–12 weeks beforehand, when – assuming you don't have a last-minute trip to Barbados planned – your skin tone will probably be similar to how it will be on the day. 'Wear a white or ivory top for your trial (or whatever colour your dress is) as it will reflect light onto your face,' Paula adds. That evening is a great time to organise a big night with friends so you can make the most of looking so good, but also see how the make-up lasts, and find out in advance if anything irritates your skin or eyes.

If your budget doesn't stretch to a make-up artist, there are still plenty of ways to get made-up inexpensively. Beyond the beauty counter idea, some brides have a make-up lesson as part of a hen night activity, meaning you've got a bunch of besties trained up to help you on the day.

If you're worried about the cost but keen on having an expert on hand on the morning of your wedding, it's worth contacting make-up artists to see if any offer cheaper rates. Many of them, too, are suffering the after-effects of the recession and may offer deals, particularly last-minute or for midweek weddings. 'It's worth asking the make-up artist for a package deal if there are a number of people wanting their make-up done, such as mums, sisters and bridesmaids,' adds Paula. That way you may be able to spread the cost.

Alternatively, you could also ask if a local beauty college runs reduced pampering or make-up deals: some will even provide hairdressing students who will do up-dos for just a few pounds (you can have a trial first to make sure you're happy). One bride told me of a trip to her nearest hair and beauty college where she found students willing to do her and her four bridesmaids' hair and make-up for £100, including a trial. It was good for the successful students' portfolios and for the bride's budget.

If you're really organised, you could even book an early-morning visit at a department store's beauty counter, such as MAC or Benefit, where the beauticians will do your make-up for you for free. Remember to buy the lipstick and anything else you might want for touch-ups.

❛ I wish I'd thought of that ...

Ben's eldest daughter Hannah married in Hertfordshire in summer 2011.

'Before Hannah's wedding my wife told me I wasn't allowed to cry during the ceremony. The reason was that I would start her off and that would make her make-up run. Leaving aside the fanciful instruction – there was more chance of me not breathing – I told her that a better and more realistic solution would be to wear no make-up. This had two other advantages – firstly I see little benefit to anyone in wearing make-up and secondly it saves money. Funnily enough, she didn't agree!' ❜

On-the-day beauty

When getting dressed in everyday clothes on the morning of your wedding, it's a good idea to put on a strapless bra if your wedding dress is strapless, to avoid red strap marks. 'Wear a loose top or button-up shirt so you won't ruin your hair and make-up when it's time to get dressed,' Paula adds. 'Oh, and don't forget to clean your engagement ring – an old toothbrush and washing-up liquid will make it shine beautifully.'

You may want to ask a bridesmaid to keep an eye on your make-up during the day, and give them a touch-up kit to look after for you, with your lipstick, eye liner, etc., in case you want to give it a boost later in the day.

Hair

If you're keen on a simple wedding hairdo, you might be happy to do it yourself, or book a great blow-dry the day before your big day or on the morning. But if you want something more complicated, you may need professional help: don't worry, though, there are options for all budgets.

Most hairdressers will price weekend wedding hair at £120 to £200, according to salon owner Anna Charalambous, who has two decades of wedding hair experience. 'The final price all depends on where you live, what you want, and which day of the week you book a hairdresser for,' she adds. 'Obviously most will be more pricey on weekends, and having hair put up takes more preparation than a hair-down style or half-hair up, so will cost more as a result.'

If hair is an area you need to trim (with apologies for the pun) from your budget, then find out if anyone in your bridal party is an expert, and again, it's worth approaching local colleges for hair students. Or make this the time you actually learn to do something impressive with your hair: lots of hairdressers run 'up-do' and blow-dry lessons where they will show you how to put your mane up, or in whatever style you want. If you go for this option, take a bridesmaid or someone else who'll be around on your wedding morning with you to the lesson – they'll be able to see the rear view better and help you out if anything goes wrong.

The budget version of that lesson is free on YouTube: there are thousands of 'how to' up-do videos on the site, such as those run by John Frieda's salon (johnfrieda. co.uk) where step-by-step tutorials cover fishtail plaits, low French rolls, 1960s beehives and more. There's a super-easy-to-replicate video on making a doughnut bun at tinyurl.com/weddingbun – and it looks really professional.

Google 'wedding hair' and you'll be face to face with thousands of images of ... 80s-style bouffants. So for market research, you may be better off ogling the dos on show at a red-carpet event like the Oscars – they're far more up to date. The scrapbooking website Pinterest is really useful too – people have put together loads of collections of modern wedding hair ideas already, so you can go and nick 'em – see, for example, tinyurl. com/pinteresthair.

But just because you're getting married doesn't mean you need a hairdo that involves hours of prep, with extensions and highlights, etc.: if you wear your hair down day to day because that's how it looks best, why pile it up on your wedding day? 'If you go for your hair up, make sure that you're comfortable with the style and have a hair trial,' says Anna. 'And as these are mostly priced per hour, doing your research will save you money. The better the ideas you have of what you want – such as from looking on the internet and in magazines – the more you will be able to talk about what you want on the final day, so avoiding wasting time, and expense.'

As for styling, square faces mostly suit hair that's been curled or waved, then put up so it doesn't look too severe, according to Anna, or, she suggests, 'opt for hair that's been pinned lower on the head or at the nape,' she adds, 'but make sure it's got some volume so that, face-on and in photos, you can see some hair. The expert view is that long faces suit hair up but with fringes to take length away from the face, round faces suit height rather than width, with pieces falling on to sides to soften – and lucky ladies with oval faces suit everything.

'If you can, organise your hair appointments so that any colour treatments or trims fit in a scheduled time slot for your wedding – the condition of your hair will make a big difference to its look and texture on the day, so ask your hairdresser if you should use any treatments or products to make it shinier, say, or fuller,' Anna adds. 'These don't have to cost much and can be done at home. And if you have any chemical services done to your hair, such as highlights or tint, arrange the timings around your big day a couple of months in advance so you don't have to have a last-minute extra treatment to prevent roots showing on your wedding day.'

It can be more relaxing to have your hairdresser come to your house or wedding venue on your big day, but if it's far from their own base you may be charged pricey travelling costs so watch out. 'Going to a salon rather than the hairdresser coming to you is usually cheaper,' Anna adds. 'But if you're still worried about affording a hairdresser on your special day, consider getting a trainee stylist. Or use accessories like hair jewels or a tiara to enhance your normal look. Alternatively, if you have a good relationship with your current hairdresser they might agree to a gradual payment scheme – it's worth asking as early as possible.'

Timings

When her bride-clients are planning their wedding-day mornings, Paula provides sample timings for the day – and here is her guide. She allows one hour of travel time from home to venue, and time for photos to be taken at home and at the venue before the wedding; adjust as necessary.

3 p.m.	Ceremony
2.30 p.m.	Arrive at venue and have pre-wedding photos
1.30 p.m.	Leave home
12.30 p.m.	Photographer arrives, sets up and takes 'getting ready shots' and bride shots
12 p.m.	Step into dress
11 a.m.	Bridal make-up
9.30 a.m.	Hair, have a snack and brush teeth before make-up
8–8.30 a.m.	Breakfast

Listen up

Music, dancing and entertainment

It's the thing that gets your guests off their seats and dancing at the reception, it kicks in when the speeches are over so the stars of your bridal party may be a little more relaxed, and it's the time of the wedding when everyone's had a little tipple and is ready to go crazy boogieing with you – the newlyweds! If you want your guests to stay till they're kicked out of the venue and their feet are killing them, let's start to think about music.

'We think – of course we would do – that music is one of the most important elements of a wedding,' says musician Mark Adelman. 'After all, once the food is eaten and the speeches made, there are usually several hours left to keep guests happy and entertained – if the band is not up to it, then unfortunately this will probably be the memory that your guests leave with – possibly before your party has even finished!'

Your first musical decision may be DJ versus band. What are the pros and cons? Well, bands are adroit at creating an amazing, dance-all-night-long atmosphere, they'll respond to the crowd on the night, put their own spin on tunes, and should build anything you want – say, you or a friend to take the mike for a particular hit – into your night. On the negative side, they are usually the most expensive form of wedding music, each band may only have a limited range of styles, they can be prickly about playing tunes they don't know or want to play, they take up a fair amount of space in the venue and could eat into dance-floor room, plus there's usually at least four of them and they'll all need looking after and feeding on the day.

By contrast, a DJ will usually play anything you want, should also react to your guests' mood, will be cheaper, will play the 'actual' versions of songs that you know and love – especially great for your first-dance song – and they take up less room. But bad DJs can end up ruining the atmosphere by looking bored and as though they're running on autopilot – possibly literally, with their computer running the show. Their music sometimes also lacks the spark and audience responsiveness of live performances.

Or there's a third alternative: you might be happy with making your own playlist and getting friends to keep an eye on an iPod linked up to a sound system – see below for more tips. This has the advantage that you get to spend some happy pre-wedding hours playing your favourite songs and testing out their danceability in your living room. The downside is you can't be sure your tunes will fit with the atmosphere all night long.

Ultimately, what you go for will depend on your priorities, wishes and budget.

If it's a band or DJ that you go for, a major piece of newlyweds' advice is that you need to trust them. If you love cheesy music – the kind where you know every word, and there's always at least one rendition of 'Summer of 69' – you should tell that to your band or DJ and they will of course build their playlist accordingly. But good DJs will also be guided by the guests' response to their music on the night, to ensure the dance floor is chock-a-block with bride, groom, their friends, family and parents' friends – usually spanning about eight decades in age. If you've picked an experienced wedding band or DJ, try not to stress too much about song choices, just let them know what you generally like.

Did you know?

If you can't make it through a film at the cinema without a loo break, spare a thought for members of the Tidong community in Indonesia, where tradition dictates that newly-married couples refrain from all loo breaks for three days and nights. They're also not allowed to leave their house during this time.

Try to ensure your entertainment also fits with your venue. An 11-piece jazz band fired up with amps is going to deafen your guests if there are only 40 of them in a small suite or marquee; likewise a single singer-pianist may get 'lost' in a huge banqueting suite. Check too that your venue meets their power requirements. No point picking a pricey band, say, if they need so much energy it causes a fuse to blow and cuts out the power for band, caterer and everyone else . . .

Which band?

As ever, recommendations are often the best starting point. Ask friends and family if they've been to a party or wedding with really great music that got everyone dancing. Suggestions from people you know aren't just a good indication of what you're going to hear – they'll also help you know the group is reliable. 'We frequently get calls from people who have been let down at the last minute by their band – the reason is often apparent when I ask what their allocated music budget is,' says Mark. 'If their band had agreed to play for them for an unrealistic fee there is always the chance that if something better/more lucrative comes along they will take it instead, and leave you in the lurch.'

Once you get some names, Google the bands to watch videos on YouTube, or find them on Facebook or MySpace. If possible, go and see them live too.

Most bands will let you slip into the back of a venue of another wedding, if the bride and groom don't mind and you dress appropriately and do it subtly. If not, see if they're playing at a public gig.

As well as liking the band's music, it helps if you like the band members. 'Our advice to brides and grooms is to have plenty of communication – email, phone calls, and meet up if possible,' Mark suggests. 'We invite couples to come and see us at one of our gigs so we can talk about their ideas and plans, and they can be reassured that we are (fairly) normal, approachable people.'

Once you've booked a band or DJ, feel free to ask for their opinions and suggestions as to what works and what may not. 'But you should be willing to listen to advice and, if necessary, change plans that you may have had your heart set on if these are actually not appropriate,' Mark adds. 'We were asked once to play a beautiful Brazilian song as an opening dance – however, I had to point out to the bride and groom that the English lyrics told the story of a couple who were no longer in love and whose relationship was now "slightly out of tune". So they came up with an alternative suggestion! Likewise, your best friend singing Adele's "Someone Like You" may not be completely appropriate, even if she did get through the *X Factor* auditions . . .

Band-booking checklist

Here's a checklist for booking a wedding band, DJ or other musician, from the experts at WeddingMusic.co.uk:

- Ask for a repertoire list and demo recordings before booking to ensure that the act is right for you and your guests. (Usually supplied online, although some bands and ensembles still use CDs.)

- Don't be too afraid to book a band without having seen them play live, provided you are happy with their demo, song list and experience. The top wedding bands tend only to play at private events because they have enough of this sort of work never to need to play pub and club events. Realistically, the only time you would be able to view such a band would be at someone else's wedding – and some bands don't encourage this. How would you feel about other couples coming to your reception just to view the band?

- Be absolutely clear as to what you want the musicians to do. One unfortunate bride wanted '(Everything I Do) I Do It for You' by Bryan Adams – from the film *Robin Hood: Prince of Thieves* – at her wedding. Her local organist didn't know the song and decided instead to play what he thought was a suitable alternative. The bride therefore found herself walking down the aisle to the strains of 'Robin Hood, Robin Hood, riding through the glen!'

Band-booking checklist

🐚 Write everything down, and ask for written confirmation from the performers. Draw up a contract or letter of engagement, signed both by you and the musicians. Specify timings, although bear in mind that all wedding receptions run late.

🐚 Don't pay a penny until you have agreed the details of the musicians' performance with them.

🐚 Once you've booked your musicians, don't be too prescriptive about repertoire. Of course the bride and groom should choose the first dance, and the pieces to be played during the ceremony, but beyond that you'll get the best out of your musicians if you leave it to their experience and expertise to read the mood and adjust their set accordingly on the day.

🐚 Call the musicians at the start of the week of the wedding to reconfirm everything.

🐚 Supply a contact phone number (such as that of the best man) in case of a problem on the way to the wedding.

🐚 Remember, musicians are people! If you look after your musicians – for example, providing a bite to eat and a comfortable room for their breaks – they'll go the extra mile for you in their performance

'Musically speaking, think about the whole evening and about the diversity of tastes and age groups you will have at a wedding – a traditional jazz band or a Deep House DJ may be your idea of fun but it's fairly unlikely that your guests will feel the same! Never be afraid to ask your musicians any questions in advance – it's essential that both you and they know what to expect from each other on the day.'

Hey, Mr DJ …

The rise of iTunes and music downloads mean DJs at weddings aren't the greasy-haired, pot-bellied old fogeys with 100 or so CD options that some once were. 'Music,' says DJ James Regal, 'is much more accessible nowadays, so couples are able to take a really bespoke approach to their wedding playlists. In the past, the idea of the traditional wedding DJ was a guy who turned up with a few flashing lights and his record collection of all the cheesy classics and big pop tunes of the moment – you were at the mercy of his personal tastes and a somewhat limited music collection.

'Now, it is so much easier to work with the bride and groom to plan the entire night around all the songs they want played. I often get asked to play some quite obscure stuff which, before the digital music revolution, would have been quite tricky to find. Now I can just search for it on iTunes or countless other music sites and have it within seconds.'

Even the guests are now getting involved in flagging up their favourite dance-floor tunes, James adds. 'At some of the weddings I've played, the bride and groom have wanted to get their guests more involved in either the music selection or even providing it themselves, so have either asked for song choices when people RSVP, or invited guests to play those songs themselves under the DJ's supervision.'

Hiring a DJ usually works out at a slice of the price of a band – as little as £300 in some areas of the UK, where the venue is all set up for music, up to around £1,000 for a bigger name who is also bringing equipment. 'Nothing,' DJ James surprisingly admits, 'really beats live music from a great wedding band, but a good DJ can still create a fantastic atmosphere. Personally, I always work several weeks or even months in advance with the bride and groom to make sure I have a full understanding of their musical tastes, what their friends like, and the age range and number of guests that will be present. Ensure your DJ knows the same details. There will usually be a few key songs that get people going and then you just take it from there.'

Money-saving DJ ideas

Think local. 'Find someone local to the venue (it's worth asking for recommendations from your venue or other suppliers if not in your area) as they may otherwise add on hefty travel costs,' says James. 'Also check that they are able to bring their own DJ set-up with them or book a venue that already has this in place, so you avoid additional hire charges.'

Ask around – you might know a DJ without realising it. 'The best way to cut back is to see if any friends or work colleagues DJ themselves or are involved in bands that play weddings,' says James. 'So many people are DJs nowadays that it should never be too hard to find someone to do the job for you for mates' rates.'

Failing that, you could knock out the cost entirely by setting up a whopping great playlist on an iPod, full of dancing songs. There will be downsides – no one to recognise if the mood has gone a bit slow-dancey or an upbeat floor-filler is needed, for example – but 'if you really can't afford to hire anyone to play music then you can go down the route of creating a massive playlist on an iPod, iPad or laptop and plugging it into the PA system,' says James.

'There are a few apps that will actually mix between songs for you so there are no gaps between tracks, such as 'djay' for the iPhone and iPad. It costs about £7 and has a decent automix feature and can pull songs directly from your iTunes library,' he says. 'It's never going to sound as good as someone mixing properly but can be a decent stopgap. Or you can also set iTunes to automix, which will give you a very basic fade-in/fade-out transition between songs, although it can sound a bit clunky. Alternatively, another app, AccuBeatMix, arranges your iTunes library in order of beats per minute, or tempo. That means you won't have a fast song suddenly switching to something much slower.

'If you want a mixture of up- and down-tempo songs, the best way to use this is to plan the night in advance and create a few different playlists that fit the progression of the event – like easing your guests into things with some slower Marvin Gaye or Motown stuff early on, and then have them doing 'Gangnam Style' as things get a bit more raucous later on . . . 'It won't always sound brilliant but it's a decent compromise.'

Top tip for DIY DJs

On average, a pop song lasts between 3 and 5 minutes, so you'd need between 24 and 40 songs to fill two hours.

Instead of having a totally autonomous laptop or iPod with a playlist, you could ask one of your mates to take nominal control. Make sure they're trustworthy and not big boozers, though.

One thing not to scrimp on is the equipment used to play the music. 'Whoever or whatever you use to play the music – band, DJ or iPod – it will all sound terrible unless you have a decent PA system,' James warns. 'If the venue has its own, make sure you get someone who is familiar with sound systems to check the spec fits what you need; if they don't, ask an expert before hiring or buying anything.'

That dance

A couple I know had their sleep ruined for weeks before the big day because the bride had a recurrent nightmare about their first dance, with all their guests' eyes on them and it all going wrong. I know a lot of people get worried about this part of the day, and I was definitely one of them. Put two elephants on their hind legs and they'd look better than my husband and me trotting around the dance floor. In a bid to avoid total dance-floor humiliation, we booked a dance lesson before our big day. Not to put on one of those choreographed first-dance numbers that go viral online now and then, but just to shuffle round the dance floor, in time, and without one of us tripping the other up and necessitating a mid-nuptials A&E visit.

I'd love to say it all changed but (with thanks to Joan in our local church hall for trying) . . . it didn't. We still can't dance. But no one laughed (too hard) on our wedding day – and believe me, however anxious you feel in advance, you'll be bouncing around on this happiness cloud that will mean you'd dance with your new husband or wife on the big night even if they were a tiger who hadn't yet had dinner. Another case in point: half an hour before her first dance, my sister-in-law begged us to join her and her new husband on the dance floor no less than three seconds after they'd started their solo first dance. But we held back because once the music started and they rocked around the dance floor, they forgot all about their worries.

Want to terrify yourselves? Check out these practically-pro first dances: Anita and Patrick, with *Dirty Dancing*'s 'The Time of My Life' (tinyurl.com/weddingdanceone), Andy and Kelly's mad medley (tinyurl.com/weddingdancetwo), Ryan and Frankie's jive (vimeo.com/41751468) and the hip-hop dance at tinyurl.com/weddingdancethree. If you want a showstopper like one of these you've probably already done a spell on *Strictly Come Dancing*, or else want to find some dance lessons. The website firstdanceuk.co.uk links up nearly-weds with dance teachers around the country.

Otherwise, if you're happier keeping it simple, you just need to work out which song to opt for. If there was a particular track playing when you met, or got engaged, it might be easy. Gemma Rogers, an experienced teacher of first dances, tells nervous brides and grooms that practice makes perfect – or at least passable. 'Move the coffee table out of the way, play the song and dance to it around your living room,' she says. 'The time you put in beforehand will make such a big difference on the day. You'll get used to holding each other and moving around together. Make sure that when you practise, the bride wears shoes similar to what she'll wear on the day and takes into account her dress and how restrictive it may be.

'Just have fun and see what happens. For some inspiration, you could watch dance shows like *Strictly Come Dancing* as well as searching around YouTube for other couples' videos. Dancing is all about enjoying yourself, so if you're seen to be enjoying it then your guests will too. If you're not confident enough to dance to the whole song, or you just don't want to be alone on the dance floor for too long, have a word with your bridesmaids or ushers and let them know that you'll signal for them to come and join you. Dancing is meant to be fun, no one will judge you – and it's your moment to shine.'

Need some help on songs? You're not alone. 'Many brides and grooms find it incredibly hard to choose music for the first dance,' Rogers adds. 'The first step is deciding on the mood you want: slow and romantic, or something a little bit more fun and up-tempo. When you have decided on the mood it's important to choose a song you both like, not just any song that is easy to dance to. Slow songs aren't necessarily easier,' she adds (maybe that's where we went wrong?).

'Also, listen carefully to the lyrics of the songs as sometimes they're not really appropriate for your first dance together as man and wife. And if you have a song that is 'your song' – maybe you heard it on your first date, or at a poignant moment – then that is probably the song you should dance to. There are very few songs that you can't dance to, or that aren't suitable, especially when it comes to your first dance. The more meaning the song has to you, the more you'll appreciate it and the more your family and friends will too.'

Some of First Dance UK's suggestions for songs for that first boogie are:

'Everything' by Michael Bublé

'Let's stay together' by Al Green

'At last' by Etta James

'Amazed' by Lonestar

'Make you feel my love' by Adele

'Greatest day' by Take That

'(I've had) the time of my life' by Bill Medley and
    Jennifer Warnes (from *Dirty Dancing*)

'One day like this' by Elbow

'Better together' by Jack Johnson

'You're the first, the last, my everything' by Barry White

'Head over feet' by Alanis Morissette

'The Muppet Show' (Theme from *The Muppet Show*)

'Murder on the dance floor' by Sophie Ellis-Bextor

'Sex bomb' by Tom Jones

'Sexual healing' by Marvin Gaye

'All out of love' by Air Supply

'You never can tell' Song from *Pulp Fiction* by Chuck Berry

Theme tune to *Coronation Street* (the couple met while working on its set)

'Lady (hear me tonight)' by Modjo

'Son of a preacher man' by Dusty Springfield (the groom's father married the couple)

'I do, I do, I do, I do, I do' by Abba

'Waterloo' by Abba

'Don't want to miss a thing' by Aerosmith

'You make it easy' by Air

'If I ain't got you' by Alicia Keys

'I Swear' by All 4 One

'Perfect day' by Allstars

There are more song suggestions at tinyurl.com/firstdancesongs and tinyurl.com/50firstdancesongs.

Other entertainment

If dancing isn't your thing, or you want some extra entertainment ideas for your wedding day, you're in luck: there are one helluva lot of options out there. As well as getting your guests out of their seats, they're a good way to encourage even those most bound up with English reserve among your party to chat to new people. For actual suppliers you'll need to seek out those in your venue's area, but here are some ideas:

Classical musicians – choir, cellist, harpist, string quartet, pianist, barbershop quartet, opera singers. There are even some vocalists who dress up as waiters and shock guests when their soup-server suddenly bursts into beautiful song.

Karaoke – if you want music and participation but nothing as formal as a traditional band, you can't up the fun stakes more than by hiring a karaoke set-up. Wedding planners also tell me it's a hot new trend for nuptials. Be warned, though, you won't be able to decide who takes to the mic, and they could sound awful . . . On the flip side, it'll be memorable . . .

Performers – whether it's belly dancing that wows you or perhaps a circus performer or stand-up comedian, they can all help receptions go with a bang.

Tribute bands – love The Beatles or Take That? Whatever your budget you're probably not gonna get them at your wedding. However, The Bootleg Beatles and Take That 2 are more attainable . . .

Magician – they'll go round the tables, pulling coins out of ears and rabbits out of hats.

Celebrity lookalikes – keep guests guessing and add a touch of fun to photos. Just make sure they're half-decent: a few of the 'Prince Williams' trying to earn a crust in this way look nothing like him.

Casino – not a mini Vegas, just a fun one where guests can while away time fluttering fake money on roulette and more. Some wedding casino providers will even let you print your photo on the fake notes, doubling up as a cool and random favour for your guests to take home.

Giant games – Giant Jenga, Connect 4, table football, Monopoly... whatever your favourite game is you'll probably be able to find someone who'll supply it in giant sizes. They're great for getting people mixing during the reception. Just don't let the boys get too competitive!

The ceilidh – Scottish dancing with direction – even those who dance like they've got two left feet have fun with this one.

Slideshow – if your venue has the capability or you can get your hands on a projector, beamed-up pics of you and your fiancé(e) on stag/hen nights or just with friends and family guarantee some laughter during the reception.

Chocolate fountain – you can snap up small ones for as little as £10, and larger ones for not much more. Ask your caterer to stock it up with fruit, marshmallows, etc. and it makes a great dessert option or wedding cake alternative. Just be careful if you're in a big white dress . . . Ditto vodka luge/ ice sculptures.

And don't forget the simple table-top entertainment ideas, like those listed on page 192, or quizzes, table name-games (where the MC or a speaker tells whole tables they have to cheer when their name is mentioned in a speech – it makes everyone actually listen), and guest books or posters that ask attendees to answer questions or give fun advice.

Amazing home-made favour ideas

Favours are another way you can unleash your DIY creativity (whatever areas it lies in) to give your guests a reminder of your day. Friends bought a job-lot of transparent pillboxes on eBay, filled them with colourful M&Ms and other sweets, tied them with ribbon and

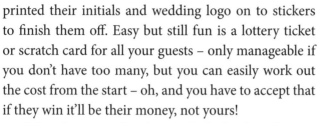

printed their initials and wedding logo on to stickers to finish them off. Easy but still fun is a lottery ticket or scratch card for all your guests – only manageable if you don't have too many, but you can easily work out the cost from the start – oh, and you have to accept that if they win it'll be their money, not yours!

Other home-made ideas include bookmarks, tea towels, CDs burned with songs from your party, little pots of home-made jam or chutney, coasters, candles, cute cardboard boxes filled with home-made fudge, sweets or little cakes or flip-flops for high-heeled guests (doubles up as a way to keep them on the dance floor a lot longer than they might in their six-inchers). You can buy tiny tubes of personalised Love Hearts direct from the manufacturer online or on eBay – 50 packs for £14 (tinyurl.com/ebaylovehearts or shop.lovehearts.com/love-hearts) – they looked very impressive.

Be wary of packaging costs: specialist wedding websites sometimes have seriously inflated prices for DIY project extras – tiny pockets of cellophane for, say, chocolate truffles or little pots for jam can be charged at £1 each, meaning the cost can soar. Instead, check out the ethnic shops on your local high street: local ethnic stores stock an amazing range of cheap packaging options.

If your guests are staying over in local hotels, it can be nice to leave them a 'welcome gift' on arrival. It doesn't have to cost a lot: ideas include filling cellophane bags with bulk-bought Quality Street or other chocolates (two big tins, a fiver each), tied with a ribbon and a 'thank you for sharing our special weekend' message. In fact, filling up some organza or cellophane bags with heart-shaped chocolates or anything else you think of and tying them with ribbon and a 'thank you' tag instantly looks very pro. Or to actually go down the pro route, you can get personalised M&Ms with your initials or a message on at mymms.co.uk. They're not cheap, (£75/1.5kg, or £2.90 for little bags), they're not going to change your life, or wedding, but they do look very cool!

I wish I'd thought of that ...

James Tracey, wedding photographer:

'One of the best wedding ideas I've seen was lottery scratch cards as favours (but sadly no one became a millionaire). The worst is the receiving line – it takes ages, makes people grouchy and it doesn't even make great photos. And although it sounds romantic, watching white doves being released is just painful. Plus the lighting of Chinese lanterns has never gone well at any wedding I've been at. Sorry everyone!'

Dietary requirements

Catering and cakes

There's a Mongolian marriage tradition that involves the bride and groom jointly killing a chicken, then gutting it to look for a lucky sign on its liver. If found, the happy couple can then set the wedding date. If not, a lot of chickens face the knife until they find a satisfactory liver.

Luckily for any squeamish brides and grooms, that's not the done thing in most British weddings: the closest most get to a chicken is the main course. The most traditional nuptial meal is a three-course sit-down affair, often with a soup starter in winter, meat or poultry main, and any dessert or wedding cake to finish. That's the so-called 'wedding breakfast': it's definitely the traditional option for a post-ceremony party, but can also be the most expensive. If this is the option you're after, the number and range of caterers out there may befuddle you. What's the right price per head? What's included, and what isn't? This chapter will help you trim the fat, if you'll excuse the pun, but still have a great wedding spread.

You might be after something quite different: many brides and grooms are now ripping up the rule book and organising catering from their favourite local restaurant, for example – a colleague did this and his guests raved about the unusual and delicious Lebanese cuisine (though you should always make sure the eatery is geared up and experienced at catering for numbers of your scale, off site). You could instead organise an afternoon tea party, or a barbecue, or serve up individual pies from a gourmet (or not!) van, or offer a relaxed fish 'n' chip meal, or finger buffet, or have a French crêpe stand, tapas, hog roast, or street-food-style kiosks like wok stations, sushi servers or hot dog stands.

The range of cuisines on offer in the UK means you're almost always going to be able to find whatever unusual idea you've thought up, and being culinary-imaginative could actually save you money as well as wowing guests who'd set themselves up for yet another portion of chicken in a cliché sauce.

Alternatively, if you want to serve up a particular meal or cuisine that you or your family are always cooking up, you might even be able to pull off a buffet meal that you/your friends/family have prepared yourselves and just hire a few servers or chefs to pull off the final touches. Be aware, though, that unless your mum is Delia Smith this could be stressful and dampen your enjoyment of the run-up to the big day. If you do go down this route, it's a good idea to keep it simple and easy to prepare ahead of time, with dishes such as huge one-pot meals like paella, or a summer buffet of cold cuts, or pies or quiches that can be frozen in advance – making sure too that you have adequate cooling and heating equipment for the food. The last thing you want is to be sick on your honeymoon, then call home and find that everyone else is too. Food poisoning is not quite what you want your wedding's talking point to be.

Generally, your catering options will be influenced by your choice of venue: some allow outside caterers, or even home-made food; others will insist you use their supplier – which will either be their in-house team or a set company or someone from a list of companies they recommend. Sometimes this latter option ends up being a great deal: venues that offer packages on a per-head basis can be good value, especially in the 'off-peak season' (see page 23). But be aware that your food choices may be more restricted as a result.

If you are booking your own caterer, it's worth doing a lot of research to ensure you've got a good one, especially as the food (and drink) will usually eat up the largest chunk of your budget. All the usual sources will be able to advise – venues, other wedding suppliers, friends and family, acquaintances on Facebook and Twitter, and online reviews. Once upon a time it was easy for wedding suppliers – be they caterers, photographers or anything else – to dupe potential clients by giving them contact details of only their most-happy former customers, but nowadays social media means you can contact other brides and grooms fairly easily, even if you don't know them, to ask for their thoughts.

Grilling the caterers

These are the questions that wedding planners advise you to ask potential caterers:

🍃 What kind of food do you specialise in? Can I see some sample menus and photos of meals you've cooked for other events? If you or a close friend or family member have not been to one of their catered dos, you might want to ask if it's possible to schedule a tasting of the kind of meal you're keen on before paying a deposit.

🍃 Even at the very first meeting, it's worth talking in depth about exactly what you want for the food on your wedding day. Canapés? Dips and salads for starter or full sit-down meal? Traditional wedding cake or cheesecake or ice-cream sundae station? What time of day do you want your meal served? Do you want a casual lunch, unusual afternoon tea or formal dinner? If you're trying to cut costs, it's important to let your caterer know. Most caterers are quite flexible and should be able to help you by suggesting cheaper cuts of meat, canapés or tableware options.

🍃 Do they only work at events that have a certain number of guests? If you're planning a small do, ask this before setting up a meeting to avoid wasting your time and theirs.

🍃 Get down to the details on pricing asap. Most caterers will have a range of prices, but ask for a detailed quote based on the foods you choose, number of courses, estimated number of guests, and any extras such as canapés, wedding cake, sweet stand, late-night snack, etc.

   – Ask for an itemised quote so you can work out the cost if you eliminate or organise certain items (such as the cake) yourself, but ensure the caterer is happy to agree.

   – Find out if they only offer a per-head rate or can also offer an all-

Grilling the caterers

inclusive deal so you know what you're paying ahead of time. If you're buying drinks, plus things like tableware, from the caterer, what's the cost?

– Does their pricing include staff, and if so, how many? Is that enough? Does the price include their work all night or does overtime become an issue if, say, the schedule slips and dessert is served late?

– Get a full quotation, in writing, and make sure it includes all the details you talked about at any meetings. Find out how much the deposit is and when it is due; ditto with the balance of the payment. Is VAT included? Are there any other extra costs that could be payable that are not included in the estimate?

– Don't be embarrassed to ask lots of questions – getting something wrong at this early stage could put the rest of your budget and other elements of your wedding that you have already organised in jeopardy. Finally, on the bill front, make sure you're happy with the cancellation policy.

Will the catering boss (who you'll probably be talking to at the first meeting) be there on the day, or does she/he have a manager standing in? If so, you might want to meet that person before booking too. If you don't have a wedding planner or MC, you might want a caterer to get involved with timing issues like liaising with the band/DJ on when to cut the cake, working out what to do if the timetable slips or guests aren't in their seats on time, etc. So check if they are happy to do this. If not, you may need to either look for an alternative caterer, find a pro MC or planner or ask an organised friend or family member to take on this role. Otherwise all the suppliers could be coming to you/your parents with questions on the day – which is not what you want!

Grilling the caterers

🍃 If the caterer is providing crockery, tables, chairs, cutlery, etc. (more likely if you're getting wed in a marquee or 'dry hire' setting such as a village hall), have you seen their supplies and are you happy with them? Who pays for breakages – and if it's you, how much would that be?

🍃 Will the caterer take on other work on the same day or weekend as your wedding and will that mean they are juggling several events? If they're a big firm that might be fine, but if not, you could be concerned that they may have too much on their plate (perhaps leaving too little on your guests'!).

🍃 Will the caterer and his/her staff happily deal with setting up your room? If it's the same venue for the ceremony and reception, how long will they need to turn it around and do they require extra staff to do so (and at what cost)? If you've got DIY details such as favours, kids' activities, etc., are they happy to lay them out for you?

🍃 Is the caterer happy to prepare special dishes for vegetarians, vegans and kids, plus cope with the dietary requirements of guests who may be kosher, want halal meat, or have allergies or other restrictions? Is there an extra cost for that? Do they provide meals for other suppliers (you'll need to feed band/photographer/videographer/MC, etc.) at a reduced rate? How much notice do they need?

🍃 Will they offer a full tasting with a range of menu ideas before the day? When will the final menu be decided (you may want this before invites go out)?

🍃 By what date will they need to know final guest numbers?

🍃 When and where will the food be prepared? Is all the food fresh, or could some be prepared in advance (if so, what)? If your caterer

Grilling the caterers

is not familiar with your venue, and it has some specific needs/problems, you might want to visit it with them before booking to ensure they can work there. At marquee weddings, for example, the caterer may have to bring their own cooking facilities. If this is the case, how much extra will it cost and has the firm done this before? Are the power supplies in the venue sufficient for the number of ovens/fridges, etc. required?

- Alcohol. See pages 165–75 for details, but you'll need to work out whether your venue, your caterer or you are providing booze for your big day. If you're allowed to provide your own supplies, find out if there's a corkage fee, ask your caterer for their costings (they could offer a good deal), and if you do decide to DIY, ask if their staff will still run the bar/serve drinks, etc., or if there's an extra fee for that. Alternatively, if your guests aren't big drinkers, you may want to ask if the caterer can do alcohol on a 'sale or return' basis, where you only pay for what is drunk.

- Ask for references, but remember to contact past customers yourself via social networking sites if you can – they are more likely to be honest that way.

- If you're keen on a wedding cake, ask for a quote and see how many people it will feed if you want it to serve as your dessert too (an easy money-saver: you knock out the costs of a whole course and can ask for a few fruit platters to go alongside it if you want). Alternatively, ask the caterer if you can bring in your own without an extra fee. (See pages 160–63 for more cake cost-cutting ideas.)

- If you've already lined up other suppliers, has the caterer worked with your band/florist, etc. before? This isn't crucial, but since they're setting up in the same space and working together all day, it can help.

Costs will vary hugely depending on the 'luxury level' of the caterer, as well as location, number of courses, nature of your meal (lasagne or fillet of beef, etc.), what else is included (many caterers will organise crockery, cutlery, tablecloths, etc., if the venue does not) and, of course, the number of people. Prices can start as low as £10 a head for a simple self-service buffet or barbecue-type meal, up to over £100 a head for top caterers serving a luxury meal.

Once you've booked a caterer, paid the deposit and enjoyed the tasting, it may ease stress later on if you can organise a meeting with them, your MC (or whoever is going to make announcements, etc., on the day) and a contact from your venue. That way, they'll all know each other and can smooth out any problems in advance. If you can't get them all in one place at one time, ask the caterer if they will meet you at the venue, if they've not cooked there before, to plan a timetable for the day. Caterers will usually be among the most experienced wedding experts in your armoury and will be able to help prevent you making unrealistic plans, such as expecting it to take five minutes to move 100 people from a ceremony room to a reception, and likewise on to dinner.

'A schedule is critical to the success of your wedding day,' says wedding caterer Daniel Gill. 'Setting the pace and style for a memorable and enjoyable celebration all stems from getting the timings exactly right. For example, make sure your reception is no longer than an hour and a half. Think about whether you want a greeting line (which will typically cause a 45-minute delay) and remember, your guests may be hungry. Give careful thought to the end of the meal, the speeches and the start of the entertainment; plan a lighting change or announcement to get the guests to join the bride and

❛ I wish I'd thought of that …

Gabriella married Fiachra in September 2012 at St Mary's Church in Berkshire, and then partied in a big field.

'My husband has a very large Irish family and we invited over 200 people, so things had to be cut back a bit. We had a buffet, rather than a sit-down meal, and bought £5 Sainsbury's Prosecco, which was fab. We bought cut flowers from a field and arranged them ourselves and I made every single piece of decoration by hand – I now hate crêpe paper and ribbon … !

My sister made us an incredible photo booth so we didn't have to hire one, I got a London taxi rather than a wedding car, and my dress cost £70. We also made ping-pong tables for our reception by putting nets across tables.

My advice is, while planning you big day, keep some things to yourselves to be a surprise on the day. People mean well but opinions can genuinely damage friendships.' ❜

groom on the dance floor and get the party started. An organised schedule will ensure that each part of your big day has the right meaning and energy, so take care to get it right.'

The cake

You know how Marie Antoinette supposedly said 'Let them eat cake'? She definitely didn't mean wedding cake. Or at least, not one baked by a specialist wedding cake supplier, because I doubt even she could afford to feed just her family on wedding cake for a year, which is a shame, as there are some absurdly gorgeous cake designs out there. But on some, the most amazing part of the cake might well be the bill.

In fact, it is fairly easy to have a beautiful wedding cake for £100 or less. If you've got a specific, intricate design in mind, you're probably going to have to go pro: sugarcraft takes a fair whack of time and effort, and if you find something super-cheap then most likely there will be a reason for it – like it'll taste of a rice cake, aka cardboard.

Far better to print off or sketch the kind of design you want and talk to local bakers, who tend to be more reasonable than wedding cake specialists, ask for recommendations, and seek out lots of quotes so you know the price you'll have to pay for the cake design that you want. When you do find a cakemaker you're happy with, look at their past work, then talk to former customers and check you're happy with the price, design and delivery date. You'll normally need to pick up the cake just before the wedding day, so ask a trusted member of your wedding party (who isn't going to forget, or nibble a sugared flower/piece of your marzipan wedding dress en route) to be in charge of this.

Alternatively, if you just want a big tiered wedding cake and aren't too fussy about the rest, or if you want something totally different from a traditional fruit 'n' marzipan fest, there are tons of other options. You can buy plain white cakes of various sizes from bakers or supermarkets: Marks & Spencer, for example, sells traditional wedding cakes either alone or in a combination of sizes, in either conventional fruit cake covered in marzipan and soft icing, or sponge filled with buttercream and raspberry jam. The top ring costs £8, medium £16, large £30 and extra-large £44; all together that would easily serve more than 140 people (and remember not everyone eats cake) or a lesser combination would be cheaper for a smaller party. It also sells extra blocks of cheaper 'cutting cakes' to feed more mouths for about £14. Stacking these on a tiered stand with simple fresh roses or other flowers in between looks brilliant (tinyurl.com/Markswedcake).

Other supermarkets often run other cake deals, especially in peak summertime. You may need to hire cake stands – local bakeries will often provide them, or you can buy second-hand stands from other brides at sites such as preloved.co.uk or on eBay.

Another idea is to ask friends and family in case there's an amazing baker or cake-decorator among them. If you feel cheeky asking for a cake, you could offer to buy the ingredients, or jot them a note saying how much you love their baking, and wondered if they would mind whipping you up a cake as a wedding gift. There's a much-admired wedding cake recipe consisting of three different bases (chocolate, fruit cake and lemon) as well as step-by-step instructions to icing and constructing the tiers at tinyurl.com/wedcakerecipe.

Stacking cupcakes can also look brilliant and these are easier to make (a couple of friends or family members could make a bunch of them so it's less work for one person, although it's best to agree the recipe and icing design first). For inspiration, pay a visit to tinyurl.com/altwedcakes. You can even make your own personalised cupcake holders (free) with the templates at tipnut.com/free-cupcake-wrappers.

It's also possible to personalise plain cakes with models of you and your other half thanks to inexpensive 'toppers' made by one of the country's sugarcraft whizzes. Some are expensive – as much as £200 – but you can buy non-edible ones (and who's going to know?) for less on sites such as cakefigures.com (£45). They'll turn into a great souvenir after the day too. Or artistic brides and/or grooms might want to have fun painting their own – Etsy sells cute wooden doll cake toppers which you can personalise for about £12 at tinyurl.com/etsytopper.

Another growing trend I've spotted at a bunch of recent weddings is serving guests the cake – or cupcakes – instead of an official 'dessert course'. And a further option, raved over at a wedding I went to last summer, is to ask lots of guests to whip up their favourite cake or brownies or other dessert, and create a cake table which will then turn into an amazing display at your reception. At the wedding I went to, each baker told the bride in advance what cake they would make, and she made little signs reading things like 'Mary's delicious apple cake' and 'Darren's famous brownies'; it meant everyone had loads of options for desserts, the bakers felt like they'd made a personal effort for the bride and groom, and they faced no extra costs for one course of the wedding meal.

Alternatively, you might want to dump the idea of a cake entirely and consider a fun dessert station instead, like an ice-cream sundae stand, with ice creams, cones, hundreds and thousands, sauces, marshmallows, Smarties and more. Or you could fill Kilner jars with loads of different cookie flavours, or have that chocolate fountain, or a pick 'n' mix station with favoured or retro sweets, or platters or a display of fruit, for fans of a more natural sugar high, or your favourite chocolates or childhood treats, or a tower of wheels of your favourite cheeses – if you're more fans of Brie than brownies.

Cheers!

How much booze to have and how to save on costs

If your caterer and venue allow you to purchase alcohol yourself, this is a big area in which you can save money. In general, most brides and grooms want to put on a good spread of booze; people expect it and their faces could look a little sour in photos if they're asked to put their hands in their own wallets all night long, from the first reception tipple to the last dance, having probably already shelled out a fair whack just to be at your big day. On a more practical level, a fair few of us Brits need some alcohol running through our veins to even think about venturing on to a dance floor and you probably want it to be full all night long. Also, after the ceremony, most will be thirsty for some sort of refreshment.

So yes, even though it's pretty common to have a cash bar for some of the evening, it's a nice idea to pop at least one glass of bubbly into your guests' hands at the reception, and have something on the tables during dinner. But the good news is, this doesn't have to cost as much as you think. Work out what you need with the help of an 'alcohol calculator' like the one at thealcoholcalculator.com – enter details of your guest numbers and what they like to drink and it'll estimate what you need to supply. So for a wedding for 100 guests, with an estimate of 20 beer drinkers and 80 wine fans, it suggests five cases of 24 cans of beer and 79 bottles of wine; there are rough prices, too, although these are in dollars.

Eleven ways to shave your booze bill (without anyone noticing)

- Avoid champagne. A glass of 'bubbles' doesn't have to be genuine champers – and for those on a budget, I'm reliably informed that a decent sparkling wine tastes better than a cheap bottle of 'real' champagne. Most caterers will pre-pour the wine into glasses ready for guests to scoop up, so only connoisseurs will notice that their glass hasn't been filled up with something that's actually come from the Champagne region of France. (Perhaps they will also be too polite to mention the fact that they are in fact drinking cava, the Spanish version, or Prosecco, from Italy.)

- Mix it up. There's no need to offer exclusively wine or champers at the reception. Ask your caterer for mixers like Buck's Fizz (orange juice and bubbles) or more unusual concoctions such as peach juice, cranberry juice, pomegranate juice or elderflower cordial. Mixing one of these with that sparkling wine will make your alcohol go twice as far – and potentially help prevent any embarrassing scenes if a few guests are a bit too, um, thirsty . . . Name the cocktail something personal to the bride and groom and you've got an individual tipple with which to wow everyone.

- However, don't have too much choice . . . Offer guests beer, wine, soft drinks and that signature cocktail and you'll keep most people happy. Don't worry about spirits or other specific drinks.

- Keep the reception short. Think of your own drinking maths: go to a bar for half an hour and you'll have one drink, possibly two. Go for an hour, especially in a bar with not enough chairs, and you'll easily knock back four drinks or more, right? Keep the reception brief and people will need a lot less booze to get by.

Do your sums. When making your bar sums, think about volume as well as price. How far will your alcohol allowance stretch? How much do you think your guests will drink in an evening? Those who are pregnant or driving home that night will consume less, for example, so you can work out a rough drink-per-head figure. After that, talk to the wedding coordinator at your venue to work out your options.

- Some venues will let you bring in your own alcohol to stock the bar, meaning you can choose what you want, and usually secure it at a much cheaper price. If so, a bar that's free to your guests might be more achievable. (See below for cheap alcohol-sourcing ideas.)

- However, if you have to pay bar prices, and they're expensive, an all-night free bar might not be an option. No one is going to think any less of you if you can't afford it, or can put up a bit of cash but not enough for the whole night. If there will be a cash bar, be sure to let people know in advance.

- For another idea, you could consider providing free wine, beer and soft drinks to guests all evening, but ask those who want to have (pricier) spirits or champagne to put their hands in their pockets.

Eleven ways to shave your booze bill (without anyone noticing)

– If you're having some guests just coming to, say, dessert and dancing or the evening celebration, it's worth thinking if there's a way of offering these guests a drink on arrival – perhaps with a waiter holding a tray of wine, beer or bubbly as they walk through the door.

Booze cruise. If you are allowed to supply your own alcohol, there are lots of ways to cut the cost. If you've time, book a booze cruise to Calais as a pre-wedding day trip to test wines and load up the car with the best ones to kick off your celebrations. The strength of the euro put the skids on this trip for a few years, but now there are bargains galore once more. The ferry is usually the cheapest way to get to France, so look up ticket prices via a ferry aggregator site such as ferrysavers.com or AFerry.co.uk. Use these to find out who operates the routes you want, and when, and how much cheaper they are at particular times of the day, week or year. Then, when actually booking, check the direct price first as doing so often triggers a saving as you avoid agency or booking fees. If you have flexible working hours or can take time

Eleven ways to shave your booze bill (without anyone noticing)

off work, weekday crossings – especially in on Tuesdays, Wednesdays and Thursdays – tend to be less expensive than weekend ones, but avoid the school holidays if possible. Be aware of HMRC's tax rules: 'When arriving into the UK from an EU country you can bring in an unlimited amount of most goods. But you transport the goods yourself; and the goods must be for your own use or as a gift.'

- **Bargain hunt.** If you're buying booze in this country, there are still ways to do so cleverly and cut the cost. Start scouting for bargains as soon as possible – if you get engaged at Christmas, for example, seek out bargains in the January sales, as long as you can keep the booze in a cool place that will prevent in from spoiling. It's also worth having a look at the offers at wine clubs and online retailers such as Virginwines.co.uk.

- **Be vino-savvy.** Remember, there's a difference between cheap wine and good wine and you'll have to do your research (including tastings, obviously – possibly one of the best bits of wed-research around), as supermarkets and wine discounters will boast about bargains even when you can actually get the same stuff from elsewhere for far less. The experts in specialist stores such as Majestic Wines (majestic.co.uk) will be able to advise you on the best deals and wines to suit your planned meal and budget – and if you're buying a large number of bottles, they may be able to cut you a deal too. The website quaffersoffers. co.uk also lists current deals at supermarkets and other

Eleven ways to shave your booze bill (without anyone noticing)

wine-sellers, as well as having extensive expert reviews which will help anyone who feels nervous about picking drinks for all their guests, courses, etc.

- Look out for bin ends. Shops are often trying to get rid of last year's stock for no other reason than they want fresh bottles on their shelves. This also means you can serve lesser-known bottles of wine, which has another benefit if you're worried about snobbery. While any vaguely wine-interested people might know that, say, a particular vineyard or vintage was going cheap, an alternative coming from, say, an Australian vineyard might be trickier for them to price.

- Bulk buy. Make the most of discount stores and cash 'n' carries such as Costco (costco.co.uk), Booker (booker.co.uk) and Makro (store.makro.co.uk) plus the likes of Aldi and its rivals (aldi.co.uk, lidl.co.uk). These often have decent deals on wine, spirits and mixers. Always try a sample before you buy a large quantity to make sure it suits your taste.

- Become a vintner. Alternatively, if you're *really* into money-saving, you could try making your own wine. Buy a kit – the very specific, extensive instructions, are fairly easy to follow. I once made some of my own red wine that was really drinkable. I admit not being brave enough to serve it at my wedding, but if you're good at it, can make the wine (or ale) in advance and find others like it too, it's an easy way to serve up booze at a fraction of the normal cost.

Invite designs, wordings, wed-sites and order of service

The invitations

Making your own wedding invitations can be a great way to save money while also wowing guests. You might think it's only possible if you have endless hours of spare time and/or very arty friends and a hefty dollop of patience, but the huge range of creative ideas out there means you don't have to be conventionally artistic. Even if you can't draw a thing (and no one ever wants to be your partner in Pictionary) you can still make a pretty good go at invites thanks to the joy of Pritt Stick, a guillotine (if you, like me, can't cut in a straight line), pretty paper (don't bother buying it . . . read on . . .) and downloading arty (free) fonts.

There are so many amazing ideas already out there that you don't even have to come up with something yourself: find a design you like on one of the blogs or sites listed below, and adapt it to suit you and your fiancé(e), and/or your wedding theme/colour scheme, etc. Another idea is to use a favourite photo or picture or other image or graphic, or pay a few pounds for a personalised 'logo' to go on the front of your invite; that way you can easily use it for a ceremony leaflet, place names, thank-you cards and/or any other parts of your big day too.

Professional wedding stationers are great places to seek out inspiration, but some will charge as much as £5 (or even more for effects like laser-cut designs) per invitation. Yes, seriously. Do the maths – number of invitees plus a bunch of extras in case you forget anyone or need to invite your 'B list' after 'A listers' can't make it, plus the cost of designing the invite, extra inserts like directions, gift list, reply slip and response envelope – and the bill will quickly hit £1,000 at a top stationery firm, even for less than 100 guests. Meanwhile, guests will put the card up on their noticeboard for, say, eight weeks, before throwing it in the bin after your big day.

So even top wedding planners admit that stationery is an easy area in which you can cut your total nuptials bill. Personalised ideas don't have to involve endless evenings cutting and gluing in front of the TV: my sister painted a tiny picture of her, her fiancé and our family dog walking on the beach. After scanning it into the computer, that picture was then printed – with the invite words above and below it – on the folded side of a piece of card, with a window cut into the front page to reveal the picture. The end result was a unique invitation that was all about them and didn't cost a bomb, but which, beyond the initial painting, didn't involve any major creative work.

If you are keen to have a longer-lasting invite and are willing to pay a little extra (or don't have that many guests) you could even print your invite on to a tea towel, placemat or coaster (see for example weddingteatowels. co.uk, or make a design and get it printed onto a coaster, etc., by a generic photo-printing firm such as snapfish. co.uk). Your invite can be kept and used for years to come.

Below are more options, depending on how much time and creative effort you want to put in or have available. All the ideas can be made more or less expensively, depending on how much time you have to source free posh papers and other tools.

Home-made invite ideas that might take a week or more of evenings to make...

Before embarking on the project of making your invites entirely by yourself, it's wise to think about what else you've got going on in your life and ensure you've enough time and patience to do so. Depending on the design and how many people you're inviting, DIY invites can take hours. And hours. Remember the extras rule: making allowances for a few mistakes, a couple of souvenir invites and space for some B-list invites, you'll want to make/order about 15–20 per cent extra – although remember that couples and families will only receive one invite, so it's not a case of one invitation per person invited. But if your wedding is fast approaching and you've still got loads to do, making your own invites might be more stress than it's worth – instead, you could consider embellishing a shop-bought card (see below). But if you've got more time and love creative projects, then wedding mags, the websites of professional invite designers, wedding magazines and blogs all host amazing ideas. Check out these for inspiration:

- ohsobeautifulpaper.com
- tinyurl.com/marthainvite

- pinterest.com/brideandjoy/amazing-invites/
- tinyurl.com/inviteideas
- tinyurl.com/inviteideas3
- hobbycraft.co.uk/Pages/Ideas/
- blog.weddingpaperdivas.com/

Alternatively, you can find lots of free, printable templates online that you can easily personalise and print on to nice paper for your own, easy home-made invites. See for example:

- downloadandprint.com/templates
- tinyurl.com/invitetemplate
- tinyurl.com/invitetemplate2

If you can, collecting materials well in advance of when it's time to make the invites could mean securing your supplies without spending a penny. You can build up a stash of amazing posh paper and decorations for free in the form of wallpaper samples, wrapping paper offcuts, fabric swatches and tiny paint samplers from craft and DIY stores. Alternatively you can also bulk-buy home-made paper from discount stores such as The Works (theworks.co.uk), Costco, local craft stores and online. Pound shops often have cute embellishments, as do a lot of craft websites, but these tend to be pricey, so keep an eye out for sales at sites such as weddingcrafter.co.uk, handyhippo.co.uk and etsy.com.

When it's time to put the invites together, why not turn it into a party? When the design has been finalised – and especially if you've successfully broken down your cardmaking into stages such as elements to stick/tie/stuff, etc. – then you could get all the parts together and invite some willing friends round. Put on some music, eat dinner and then spend a few hours cutting/sticking/calligraphing the invites until they're finished. Working with friends, you'll probably be able to get them all organised in one or two fun evenings.

Quicker shop-bought ideas

Pretty ready-made invites are available from the likes of Marks & Spencer (tinyurl.com/MandSinvite), Paperchase (tinyurl.com/paperchaseinvite), VistaPrint (tinyurl.com/vistainvite), Confetti (confetti.co.uk) or Hobbycraft (direct.hobbycraft.co.uk/shop/weddings). If possible, start looking for the cards themselves as early as you can: you might find a stack on offer in the midwinter sales as shops make room for Christmas stock, for example.

Easy PC ideas

Brides or grooms who prefer IT-based creativity can make pro-looking invites via a computer by matching a neat design with a cool font – there are loads of free ones online, so don't restrict yourself to Apple or Microsoft's stash. Dafont (dafont.com) has thousands of free fonts for easy download, and if you use the same typeface for invites, any ceremony leaflets, direction signs around the venue, 'save the seat' signs or anything else involved in your big day, it will all match.

Using a personalised stamp and an old-fashioned ink pad can be another cool basis for a DIY invite, or to liven up a plain shop-bought card. For about £20–£25 Stamps Direct (tinyurl.com/personalstamp) will turn any logo or artwork, such as initials and wedding date, or a graphic of the two of you, into a stamp. The software at tinyurl.com/englishstamp also lets shoppers design and buy their own stamp online. Or you can pick one of the established designs and get a bargain stamp with your names on for £5 at tinyurl.com/stampingallday.

Stamps can also be used on all the extra parts of wedding stationery if desired, for example by slicing up ivory card into small rectangles, folding them in half, stamping on one half and writing the guest's name on the other for an easy place card.

Other fun ways to spruce up plain invites include ribbon – sticky-backed ribbon is easiest, and cheaply available from the likes of simplyribbons.com (it has really good sales, so look out for them) or fantasticribbons.com – and buttons. There are often interesting one-offs on sale cheaply at charity shops or markets, and a glue gun (which costs under a tenner at WHSmith, Hobbycraft and local craft shops) can then be used to stick them on to invites. Scraps of fabric such as lace or silver or gold threads with delicate beads can also work well.

Calling in the pros

If you do opt to go to a professional invite designer, quotes for an all-inclusive deal, covering not just the invitations themselves, but place names, escort cards or table plan, orders of service, thank-you cards and any other stationery may be cheaper. If the designer won't cut you a deal on that, you may be better off asking if they will give you a PDF of design work if you buy the invitations from them, so you can then print it on to your own thank-you cards, etc., if desired.

Wealth warning!

If you can avoid it, don't spend too much on the postie. Just popping a postcard in a postbox seems to cost a fortune nowadays, but the cost adds up with weight so try not to make invites too big or heavy: the weight of layers of paper, stickers, buttons, inserts, etc. can quickly tot up. In order to use Royal Mail's cheapest stamp – whether posting first or second class – the envelope has to be a maximum 240mm in length, 165mm in width, no more than 5mm thick, and weigh no more than 100 grams. It's even more important if you've got invites heading overseas. Don't forget the envelope: lined or extra-thick paperweight envelopes are heavier than you think.

The wording

More than any other part of the invitation, the wording will obviously be entirely personal to you. Not just because it will – duh! – have your names on as bride and groom, and your timings, venue, etc., but because it will reflect the nature of your big day. If your wedding is a formal, traditional affair, the invite will probably be worded in that way, and likewise if it's more of a casual bash. Sometimes the wording also reflects who is paying for the majority of the day – you and your other half, or bride's parents, both parents, etc.

Other details you may want to give to guests include timings of the whole day, location of ceremony and/or reception and the dress code. You might also want an insert with gift list information, maps and directions and RSVP details – or you could provide these via a wedding website (see below).

Sample wedding invite wording:

Option 1: formal wedding, bride's parents inviting:

Mr and Mrs Bear
request the honour of the presence of
'guest's name'
as
their daughter Ginger
marries
Owji Snuffs
at 3 p.m. on Saturday 25 August 2012
at Westminster Abbey, London
followed by a reception at
Buckingham Palace, London SW1 1AA
Black tie
Carriages at 11 p.m.
RSVP by 15 April

Option 2: both parents invite

Maple and Golden Syrup together with Treacle and Tarragon Tart
invite
'guest's name'
to celebrate the marriage of
Ginger
to
Owji
at 3 p.m. on Saturday 25 August 2012
at Westminster Abbey, London
followed by a reception at
Buckingham Palace, London SW1 1AA
Black tie
Carriages at 11 p.m.
RSVP by 15 April

Option 3: bride and groom invite

Ginger and Owji
invite
'guest name'
to celebrate their marriage
at 3 p.m. on Saturday 25 August 2012
at Westminster Abbey, London
followed by a reception at
Buckingham Palace, London SW1 1AA
Black tie
Carriages at 11 p.m.
RSVP by 15 April

There's no 'set' invitation wording: it's all about you (or your parents, kids, etc.) expressing a wish for others to join you on your special day. Couples who already have children sometimes word their invites as coming from their kids, e.g. 'Zoe and Daniel invite you to the wedding of their parents'. If you're worried about details or formalities, check out invitationconsultants.com/sw-main.aspx: it's an invitation company that has thought of every possible invite option (including divorced parents, second marriages, post-ceremony-only guests, commitment ceremonies and even rhymes) with sample wordings.

Before posting …

Check you've included all the details you want to, such as the venue, time, place, gift list info, RSVP information and possibly also directions to the venue(s) and local accommodation details. Those making a wedding website (see below) should check they've written its URL correctly on the invite, and those making an insert with extra details should check that it's in every envelope. You might want to supply RSVP cards and envelopes too, or just set up an email address (gingerandowji@ gmail.com, say, or gingerandowjiaregettingmarried@... etc). If you're going down the e-route, remember to give a phone number for those few who are not online. If you're asking people to email or phone through their responses, remember to ask guests to supply any relevant dietary requirements.

Wherever you make or source your invites from, you might want to organise some 'thank-you' cards with the same design too. That way, you'll be able to start responding to people's gifts as soon as they send them, and not have a mountain of writing to do when you get back from honeymoon.

Place cards and table numbers

If you have a wedding theme, place cards and other stationery are the areas to go crazy with it! For a seaside-themed wedding, for example, you could collect bits of driftwood or shells, and anyone with nice handwriting could then make place cards for guests. Other fun ideas for DIY place cards include origami, luggage labels, and green apples or other fruit with names pinned or tooth-picked in. Take inspiration online: the real weddings on blogs like rockmywedding.com host thousands of ideas.

Table names/numbers are another cheap way to personalise your wedding. Don't feel you need to stick to boring numbers – naming your tables after something else is much more memorable and an excellent ice-breaker too. I've been to weddings where couples named tables after special places they'd been on holiday or lived together, films they both loved, and even the twelve things they couldn't understand the other one liking!

Other nice table-name ideas are things that go together: peanut butter and jam, salt and pepper, cookies and cream, etc. And if you're feeling adventurous and reckon your guests are up for a bit of a game, you could put one half of the combo on the table plan or escort card, e.g. 'salt', and make the guests track down what their table might be ('pepper')! Song titles that you both like, random numbers illustrated with photos of you and your fiancé(e) at that age, famous couples, places you're visiting on honeymoon could also be used. There are lots more ideas at tinyurl.com/tableplanning. Another bonus is that naming tables after places rather than numbers is a great way to avoid upsetting Great Aunt Zelda: she won't realise she's persona non-favourite on table 17 if it's called something non-hierarchical!

A cheap way to show off the table names once you've made them is by propping them up in charity shop photo frames (avoiding identical ones looks retro) or you can buy a pack of four vintage-style frames from Ikea for £2.

The place names showing where guests should sit can easily be imaginatively jazzed up too: slate roof tiles can be snapped up for pennies from builders' merchants, then just chalk on guests' names. Any kids at the wedding can then use the slate as a blackboard later on to stave off boredom during the speeches.

Wed-sites

A really easy way to save money on invites – but still wow people with all your wedding details – is to create a wedding website with all the basic who/what/wheres (plus, if you want, a whole lot more than would fit on an invite, such as the story of how you met, photos, lift-share offers, etc.) and email all your guests the link. This might be impossible – if you've a lot of older guests, say, who aren't au fait with the internet – or might not be what you want: a lot of people love the souvenir element of an invite through the letterbox. But even so, you can still create a wedding website with extra details, saving on the effort and expense of invite inserts about gift lists, transport details, local accommodation, etc, or just as a way to give people a sense of what your big day will be like.

If you're not convinced about just how impressive this can be, check out jessandruss.us or tiffanyandzach.com or jennyandgrayden.com, or loads of excellent examples at tinyurl.com/awesomeweddingwebsites. These all demand a serious amount of web know-how, but you can easily set up your own wedding website, for free, without much IT nous at all. Do so by using one of the many free website-creation sites out there, such as mywedding. com, gettingmarried.co.uk or webeden.co.uk. If you fancy pushing the boat out, you can buy a domain ('gingerandowji.com', for example) which will only cost about a fiver for a year (and that's all most will need it for!), and may be easier to remember, and to fit on invites. If you want to buy your domain, or just see if your names are available, check out a hosting site like godaddy.com.

What to put on a site? It's best to keep it basic – welcoming guests, perhaps relaying your excitement with a countdown till the day (the sites offer this automatically so there's no need for advanced maths ...), giving driving/transport instructions, gift list info and maybe a 'contact us' form to link up guests who might need lifts. If you fancy it, a 'story' page telling guests how you met and posting pics of those in the wedding party can be fun. If desired, you can also use the site after your wedding day to post photos and memories and ask guests to post their own snaps.

Most of the website-making sites work in the same way, and Henry Lewington, Managing Director of WebEden, explains what to do. 'To get started, you'll need to enter your personal and wedding details to open an account, and you'll then be guided through a simple step-by-step process. This begins with choosing your favourite template from a huge selection provided, then, using simple drag-and-drop software, starting to add your pages.'

Commonly, for a site that goes live before a wedding you might want to start by creating the following pages:

- Homepage – the first welcome page, letting people know they've reached the right place.
- Our wedding – details of when and where the wedding will take place, map of how to get there.
- Places to stay – details and links to local hotels and guesthouses.
- Gifts – any requests for gifts and/or link to pre-specified store wedding list.
- Gallery – to be created after the wedding with all the great images from the day.
- RSVP – for guests to respond, perhaps with a tick

box asking for dietary requirements and/or even a slot for music requests.

🌿 And so on – you can add as many pages as you like.

Don't forget photos. If you've had an engagement shoot included in your photo package, that'll probably have given you lots of picture options, otherwise people always love silly photos or baby ones. Can they guess who is the bride and who is the groom?! 'The making of any great website is in the images and, even though the best images and videos are likely going to be taken on the day itself and can be uploaded after for people to come back to, it's worth adding in some images of the couple throughout the site right from the start,' Henry adds.

The next step is to hit 'publish' and your site is live. Some sites allow you to password- protect them (a good idea if you're worried about gatecrashers accessing your big-day details!), so you can just give the password to those you want to have access to the website.

Once the honeymoon is over, you can create a gallery of your favourite photos. It means those living far away can see your snaps easily, 'and visit them at their leisure, going through each image in minute detail or skipping through until they find the ones of them doing the conga,' Henry adds. 'Couples sometimes also choose to upload personal words from their marriage vows or great videos of the most memorable parts of the day.'

Ceremony leaflet or order of service

Once the invites have been organised, some brides and grooms like to add to their wedding stationery to-do list by tackling a ceremony leaflet or order of service. They're not crucial – all that info is really for the bride and groom, an officiant and witness, so it's all relative – but while the ceremony will be an amazing moment for you, it'll likely be a bit more mundane for guests who've probably seen it all before a fair few times, so something to read can be nice.

If you're having a religious ceremony, the order of service can be used to explain what's happening, especially if some of your guests are from a different or no faith and might not know what to expect. It might also list the words of your hymn choices (to avoid mumbling . . .). For civil ceremony leaflets, you might want to explain the order of events and tell your guests about any meaning behind reading choices. For both types of ceremony, it can be nice to list the 'VIPs' in your bridal party, and perhaps provide details of who they are, plus name your music choices. Some brides and grooms also list the timetable and location details (whether it's another venue entirely or just another room) for the rest of the day.

If the info covers more than one piece of paper, folding a sheet (or more) of A4 in half like a booklet, then using a hole punch to make two half-holes (like slits) on the edge of the folded edge means you can then insert a piece of ribbon through the middle and tie it in a bow. Or there are lots of other templates at tinyurl.com/ceremonyleaflet – including A4 scrolls that you can roll up and tie a ribbon round, and foldable pages. Another idea can be found at tinyurl.com/ceremonybooklet.

A four-page ceremony leaflet might consist of:

Front page: name of bride and groom, date and location of wedding.

Page two: a 'who's who', usually including bride, groom, officiant, musicians, parents, best man, bridesmaids, flower girls, page boy, ushers and anyone else involved in the service or processions.

Page three/four: order of service, including music, readings, prayers, etc.

The only other stationery you might want to whip up is a sign or two for the venue (if it's sprawling), menus (either with or without a list of the evening's events), name cards and escort cards. For simplicity, printing off all guests' names in the same font and colour as your invite is a really easy route to smart name cards.

There are lots of easily printable templates for menus, ceremony leaflets and more at:

- tinyurl.com/menutemplate
- tinyurl.com/tableart

☞ Or, if you are marrying somewhere hot (or hoping it will be) check out this time-consuming, but very pro-looking, DIY leaflet: fan design at tinyurl.com/faninvites

Notepads

An easy idea to bring a grin to people's faces as they sit down for your wedding meal is setting little notebooks in the places of all engaged guests, in case they see or think of anything that they want to remember for their own upcoming wedding day. A couple I know who had a small wedding spent their evenings in the weeks leading up their day writing personalised messages about each guest – saying things like: 'Sam on your left once fell into the river in Oxford while punting, and Sarah on your right owns an eight-foot-high Aztec bow and arrow. Ask her about getting it through Heathrow's security.' It made it easier for guests to get to know each other. It was a big old effort – and is probably only doable if your wedding party is fairly small – but the stories acted as a great ice-breaker when everyone sat down.

Alternatively, if you're worried about tables of people who don't know each other getting on, think about providing some table games. You could buy or make quizzes or trivia packs, or make funny crosswords or wordsearches based on you as a couple or your venue, family, etc. Or you can buy (customised) ready-made versions from sellers like etsy.com/shop/KreativeCupcake for £12. DIY crosswords (or just printed black and white photos of the bride and groom) could also be used for canapés – little cones of fish and chips, for example, can be contained in them.

Flower power

Working with florists, saving on costs, finding alternatives

They can transform even the most dull-looking venue and be the finishing touch to a bride's look – and there are more ideas and options for flowers at a wedding than petals in Kew Gardens. Traditionally anyone organising their big day's flowers would head straight for a professional florist. Nowadays, though, some brides, grooms and/or their friends and relatives are opting to create their own centrepieces, bouquets and/ or buttonholes. It's not just a money thing – although mentioning the 'w' word at a florist definitely *can* see your bill shoot up. Instead, some nearly-weds love the idea of growing and picking flowers from a loved one's (or their own) garden, or selecting and arranging their own blooms from a local nursery or flower market, to add an extra dose of meaning to their wedding day.

It's not just a question of deciding between DIY or pro flowers. There are totally different, non-floral decorative ideas and the many alternatives (see below) will depend on how you want your venue to look, your budget and how much spare time you – or whoever's willing to do the flowers for you – have. If you're short of it, don't kill yourself with home-made flower arrangements; if you find a good florist, they will always be able to work out something within your budget, whatever it is. And whatever route you go down, there are some easy money-saving ideas.

Here's the first: whether selecting flowers yourself or talking through options with a florist, blooms that are in season will look more natural and in keeping with your wedding, last longer than imported blooms, and most likely be cheaper too. See below to find out what flowers and greenery are in season when. The same is true if you're getting married overseas: picking a local flower that reflects your surroundings will also often be a cheaper option.

If your venue has amazing gardens or even just one beautiful floral border, using it as a backdrop for photos or even a part of the reception, if dry and warm enough, is a free route to wonderful wedding-day blooms. Or, if there's another wedding at your reception or ceremony venue on the same day, speak to the other couple about sharing arrangements – if you can agree on colour and style, you could both save hundreds of pounds.

Alternatively, if you're having two different wedding venues, one for the ceremony and one for the reception, it's a good idea to ensure any flowers arranged at the church or register office are portable and can be reused at the reception. Balls of blooms or teardrop-sized hanging arrangements – such as are often found at the end of church aisles at C of E or Catholic weddings or on the canopy (chuppah) used at Jewish ceremonies – can be rehung or re-laid on the top table at a reception, for example. But if you're hoping to do so, ask your florist or arranger about the dual role from the start, because they may need to be put together in a specific way.

'Concentrate your ideas and budget on the main things, like bridal flowers, table pieces, the church entrance, or chuppah for Jewish weddings,' suggests florist Kelly Rawlinson. 'Guests focus most on these, so don't worry about the staircase, etc. – people will spend the day with you and won't be looking at the fireplace! But be aware that if you decide to get married around Valentine's Day, Christmas or Mother's Day, then flowers will be more expensive – it's not the florist that puts the price up, but the flower wholesalers.'

Before meeting any florists, try to think about the kind of blooms you want. The internet is an easy place to look for floral ideas – here the Pinterest site comes into its own as thousands of brides have already compiled scrapbooks of floral wedding pictures, including every colour scheme and concept you can imagine. It's easy to use these, plus inspiration sites such as:

- tinyurl.com/magflowers
- myweddingflowerideas.co.uk
- pinksweddings.com/wedding-flower-galleries

Wedding magazines often have good floral montages, and there's even a specialist publication, *Wedding Flowers* magazine (seriously), which has loads of ideas in every colour scheme – many are pricey but they can at least provide good inspiration.

So rip out pictures of ideas you like, and print off pics from Pinterest, and take them along to florists so you can ensure the two of you are on the same wavelength from the start, and they'll be able to offer you an accurate quote for the types of arrangements that you want. 'Florists know that every bride and groom wants something that looks beautiful and classy and not like the kind of arrangement you can pick up from a petrol station,' Kelly laughs. 'We also know what works best for giving you that look, and keeping within reasonable workable budget. My biggest tip to any bride or groom is to tell your florist your budget from the start – a good one will always be able to work to your budget; they will advise you what flowers are best and offer value for money, and where to concentrate with decorations.'

For the bride's bouquet, Kelly has a budget warning: the more complicated the design, the more expensive it will be. 'A fully wired, shower bouquet takes a lot longer to make than a hand-tied bouquet or posy, so would cost more because of the extra labour involved.' Wired bouquets usually cost more than £100, whereas hand-tied bouquets can be less than half that. Here's where modern flower arrangements do the budget bride a favour, though: those huge, trailing, teardrop-shaped bouquets look old-fashioned right now, especially when compared with the glamour of a tight ball or bouquet of amazing roses, which also tend to be cheaper.

Going back to the earliest traditions, historians reckon the first people to have wedding flowers were the Greeks, who made garlands for brides to wear on their heads. These kinds of wreaths are making a comeback (they are particularly stunning when brides have their hair down), but what's important is that you go for whatever makes you feel happiest and at your best.

On the tables, be realistic, says Kelly. 'If you are having a small function, with fewer than 10 tables, keep the design for any table centrepieces small – anything too big will not only be costly but together they could look OTT in the room. And try not to overload the table with petals or candles – they can take away the impact from a centrepiece.'

If you're struggling with costs, keep it simple: a single, large-headed flower, like a big white rose, in a slim cylindrical vase (or the same in two or three vases, if affordable) set on a mirror plate (maybe surrounded by flickering tea lights) can look simple but elegant. Mirror bases also make smaller arrangements look larger. Another way to cut the cost is by providing your own glassware; some brides collect prettily-shaped jam jars, glass milk bottles, or vintage china teacups and pots: filling them with wild-looking flowers gives an amazing summery or vintage look.

As for the bridal party, think practically. If you're having young kids as bridesmaids, don't expect them to haul around a heavy hand-tied bouquet even just for the ceremony. 'Consider single flowers rather than a posy – not only does it work out cheaper but often small children find holding something large uncomfortable,' Kelly adds. 'Or you could ask your florist to add a few flowers to a teddy, wand or basket – in my years of wedding experience I've found that children are more interested in holding these and less inclined to pick the flowers apart!'

Table decorations

'The most creative ideas come from the couple themselves,' says wedding photographer Julia Boggio. 'So if you're looking for ideas, think about what you both like. Where did you meet? What have been your best holidays? What do you do in your spare time together? See if there is anything from these experiences that can help you add fun details to your wedding. One couple I photographed loved playing games, so they created a range of games to leave on the tables during the reception, like Trivial Pursuit cards with questions about the couple and the guests. One table had a contest to see who could make the best dolphin out of Play-Doh.'

Choosing flowers

The actual blooms you choose will depend on the look you're going for on your big day: different frosty, cream tones often give a sleek, glamorous look, soft pastels can be really romantic, while bright tropical flowers give huge impact. But, again, thinking seasonal will help your flower arrangements fit in with your day and come in on budget. In general, the best-value flowers all year round are, according to florists:

- Roses
- Gerbera
- Lisianthus
- Freesias
- Singapore orchids

Florist Kelly's very simple introduction to what's in season when:

Spring: tulips, freesia, daffodils, hyacinths, lily of the valley, cherry blossom, agapanthus, hydrangea, anemone.

Summer: peonies, hydrangea, roses, phlox, delphiniums, stock, sweet pea, agapanthus, iris, lilies.

Autumn: berries, gerberas, hydrangea, fruits, calla lilies, alstroemeria, dahlia, sunflower, lilies.

Winter: roses, tulips, amaryllis, freesia, hydrangea, cymbidium orchids, Singapore orchids, lisianthus, narcissi.

Flowers and their meanings

Ever since Kate married William with sweet william in her bouquet, there's been another element to flower-picking: what the blooms mean. There's a full list of practically every flower and its representative meaning at tinyurl.com/flowermeanings. Some of the most common are:

Amaryllis – pride
Camellia – excellence/steadfastness
Chrysanthemum – hope
Daisy – innocence
Freesia – calm
Gladioli – sincerity
Heather – good luck
Hyacinth – loveliness
Hydrangea – boastful
Jasmine – good luck
Lily – virtue
Orchid – ecstasy
Rose (red) – love
Rose (white) – charm
Tulip – love

Those flowers cover most of the traditional options, but don't feel you have to restrict yourself to what everyone else is picking. Buttonholes don't have to be roses, for example: tulips, calla lilies, anemones, freesias and more can all look amazing.

At any time of year you could consider including a few extras to your flower arrangements to add impact, make the actual blooms go further or fit in with your theme, such as raffia fruit in autumn, twigs/snow for winter, feathers for spring and summer, or individual items that fit with the theme for your big day, such as fabric butterflies or tiny jewels. 'Prop' ideas often look amazing: flowers displayed in birdcages, a flat wall backdrop of flowers (or wild grasses) behind the top table, and garden-themed, natural-looking flower arrangements such as those made in the shape of a bird's nest.

I wish I'd thought of that ...

Kate married Charlie at Saint Hill Manor in West Sussex in August 2012.

'We got the flowers wholesale as our venue's event planner could do that, and we bought seriously cheap vases from Ikea and some cheap white pebbles and did our own flowers.

My advice is, if you are really picky about what you want and are going to do a lot yourself, give yourself enough time to plan it, and make the big decisions like location, date and dress as early as possible.'

How to find a florist and what to ask

🌀 Like everything related to finding a supplier, recommendations are often the best route to a top florist. Ask friends and family if they've seen amazing flower displays at a wedding, corporate function or elsewhere, or look up reviews and references to florists on Facebook. Alternatively, your venue may be able to suggest some – it's always good to deal with people who are familiar with a particular place's nooks and crannies.

🌀 When you go to meet a florist, take along pictures, whether they're on your iPhone Pinterest app (see above), ripped out of bridal magazines, or backdrop shots from friends' big days. Taking images of flower arrangements you've seen and loved will help you find out if they're doable around the time of your wedding. It'll also make it possible to get a more accurate quote.

🌀 Other things to remember to take: pictures of your wedding dress, venue, theme/colours and number of people in your bridal party who will want/need bouquets or buttonholes.

🌀 Most experienced wedding florists will have books full of photos of arrangements they've done for other weddings. Pore over them! Make sure they're up to date, as well as covering all aspects of big-day floristry that you want to order – not just bridal bouquets, for example, if you're also looking for table centrepieces. Ask roughly how much the arrangements that you like cost.

🌀 Check out real-life examples too. Most florists will whip up a quick sample for you at the first meeting; all pros

How to find a florist and what to ask

should offer to arrange a proper mock-up of centrepieces a couple of months before your big day. Before booking, you may want to double-check that their flowers all look fresh, vases are clean and sparkling, and the arrangement makes the best of them both. Some florists may even let you have a look at their work set up at a venue before another wedding kicks off.

🌿 Find out what the florist could do for your budget – remember to include all the aspects you want, possibly including bridal bouquet, bridesmaids' bouquets or posies, buttonholes for the groom, ushers, fathers of the bride and groom, table centrepieces and any other ceremony or venue decorations you'd like.

🌿 Ask if the wedding flowers you're being shown are done by the actual florist you're meeting and would have on your day – usually there are several florists working in one shop, so if you've seen something you love of a florist's past work, especially if it's unusual, ensure it's something that the person you're dealing with can replicate or reinterpret.

🌿 If the florist is not already familiar with your venue, will they visit it in advance?

🌿 If you have more unusual ideas, such as decorating a swing in your venue, or you want flowers for your hair/ the wedding cake, etc., are they happy to carry this out?

🌿 Ask if a quote is complete, or if they charge any extra fees, e.g. VAT, travel expenses, hire charges or collection fees

How to find a florist and what to ask

for glassware, tea light holders, urns, stands, etc. If they do charge hire costs, can you provide your own glassware instead, if necessary? Or will the florist do arrangements that don't need glassware?

🌸 What's the policy if anything hired gets broken?

🌸 Can guests take centrepieces home (if that's what you want) after the big day? Florists will never take the flowers back afterwards (you've paid for them!) but some arrangements may be difficult to transport without the glassware that the florist will want back.

🌸 Ask if the florist is happy to transport your ceremony flowers to the reception venue, if you've got two separate ones.

🌸 Ask if they take more than one wedding booking per day. This may not be a problem if the florist has a big team or your order is small, but even so you may want to know in advance.

🌸 When will the flowers be delivered? If the bride is getting ready at home or away from the ceremony venue, for example, she may want her bouquet delivered there; likewise the groom, ushers, etc., with their buttonholes.

Most florists will ask for a deposit – of 10 per cent to 25 per cent – to secure a booking, and then will usually want payment of the full balance a few weeks before the wedding date.

DIY arrangements

If you're doing your own flowers – or have a friend or family member helping you out – it's a good idea to have a trial run. 'Bear in mind that you will be under stress and short of time in the run-up to the wedding – testing your ideas first will help you work out what to do and how long it takes,' says Kelly. 'Work out where you're going to source your flowers well in advance – most markets are wholesale only so you may need to buy your flowers from a local florist.' Some local florists run workshops where you can learn to make your own arrangements, table centrepieces, etc. – if you love flowers, you could even ask your bridesmaids to book on to a course with you for your hen do.

For accessories, eBay and other sites often see newly-wed brides selling things they have used for their own big days, such as tea lights, lanterns, vases, etc. There's even a specialist site, sellmywedding.co.uk, which focuses on the idea that 'someone's something old could be your something new'. It has a huge range of vases, mirror cubes, centrepieces and more.

'Get others to help you with arrangements – invite all your friends round and make a night of asking them to all tie small bundles of herbs which you could add to napkins,' says Kelly, 'or make small bowls of floating flowers that you can place around your venue – they're very easy to do and transport. If you get stuck, ask a florist for advice – we will always help as much as we can.'

If you can, ask that friendly florist, or specialist floral market traders, for some tips about transporting and storing the flowers too: some are best stored in a fridge, some in cellophane, some will be more thirsty than others, and some may need to be left to open in advance. Plus, some flowers shouldn't touch food or skin, so make sure you know what you're dealing with! Most arrangements will need to be made up on the morning of a wedding to prevent them drooping or shedding; some will need to be arranged with Oasis, wire or at least correct-sized vases to help the flowers look their best all night long.

> ## ❛ I wish I'd thought of that …
>
> *Ben married Cat in Watlington in Oxfordshire in December 2012.*
>
> 'We decided to embrace the Christmas spirit and have a red, gold and green colour theme. We had red tablecloths, gold baubles and we had family and friends picking ivy for a week beforehand to string around the marquee, up the candelabras and in the church. Looked amazing and completely free. The experience of getting family and friends to decorate the venue the day before was a fantastic bonding experience for us too.' ❜

Alternatives to flowers

Nowadays not many brides are going to need flowers to improve their own personal smell – or that of their venue – as they might have done in the old days (one of the fabled reasons for wedding blooms). So flowers are really only at weddings to help make a room look beautiful, and have the same function for the bride and bridesmaids (bouquets), groom, fathers of the bride and groom and ushers (buttonholes). For today's weddings, there are plenty of alternatives that can help you do just that as well as surprising your guests.

Kooky alternatives to traditional bridal bouquets, for example, include bunches of 'flowers' made of beautiful buttons or brooches, feathers, clutch bags, fans, origami, sea shells, candles (usually in glass lantern containers: you don't want to be a bride-on-fire), parasols, or even bunches of fruit, sweet or lollies – for inspiration check out:

- tinyurl.com/altbouquet
- tinyurl.com/altbouquet2
- tinyurl.com/altbouquet3
- tinyurl.com/altbouquet4
- tinyurl.com/altbouquet5

The benefit of bouquets of fabric flowers and buttons is that you can keep the bouquets as they are forever, as an amazing souvenir, unlike flowers which, however well they are dried, will never be the same as in full bloom.

As for flower alternatives around the room, candles can make amazing centrepieces – they come in hundreds of shapes, sizes and colours, can float in bowls of water with rose petals or be held up in candelabras (check out charity shops). Ikea stocks really cheap candles or check out pound shops and online stockists such as candleking.co.uk. You could also float flower heads in water (coloured with dye to match your theme if you want) in fish-bowl type vases, as Kelly suggests above, which can look simple but professional. As can pot plants (you might want take them out of their brown plastic tubs and re-pot: the galvanised silver buckets you can get cheaply from pound stores and gardening chains look lovely), which have the added benefit that you can ask some of the guests to take them home as a gift.

Silk flowers aren't for everyone but could be worth checking out. There are some amazingly realistic silk blooms out there, and they'll be less hassle to arrange in advance than real flowers as well as being cheaper. You can find a wide range at stores like Ikea and Dunelm Mill: tinyurl.com/ikeasilkflowers and tinyurl.com/ dunelmsilkflowers but may also find deals locally and online.

Other décor ideas include bunting. Either buy it from a site like Etsy, eBay, sellmywedding or one of the many specialist bunting stockists – seriously, there are loads of em! – or anyone adroit at using a sewing machine could whip some up for you if you've tracked down some pretty material. At a teacher's wedding last winter, all the kids in her class had written cute 'good luck' messages on rings of vintage paper that were pasted into a pretty paper chain by the school's art teacher. Other wow ideas spied on wedding blogs include hundreds of origami cranes and butterflies (check out the beauty of tinyurl.com/origamibirds and tinyurl.com/origamibirds2).

Photos are an easy way to personalise your venue: at a marquee wedding where there was an ugly bar at the back of the room, a bride I know draped and clipped velvet material on top of it, then hung twine over it, like a washing line, and used tiny wooden pegs (50 for £2 on eBay) to hang photos of her and her groom as babies, with friends and family, and at their engagement party, meaning most of the guests popped up in one snap or another. Other ideas include making a photo collage to hang at the reception (or on an easel), and silly or baby photos of guests as place or escort cards.

There are loads of free and easy printable ideas to jazz up tables, reception and the venue at offbeatbride. com/2012/06/diy-wedding-printables. Its links include place mats for guests with food allergies as well as props if you want to make your own DIY photo booth, such as funny signs and crazy moustaches/lips/silhouettes that you can glue to sticks or straws for people to have photo fun with. Then there are patterns for fabric bunting if you or a friend fancy making some to give a vintage look or spruce up a plain venue, admission tickets for a movie-themed event (great place cards), 'just married' banners, fun flags and straw ideas for reception drinks, templates to make your own cupcake wrappers, origami, favour bags, fortune cookie ideas, and more guest book templates.

You can also find thousands of DIY wedding ideas elsewhere online: check out sites like weddingchicks. com/category/wedding-chicks/diy-templates/ (the site offers free printables such as save-the-date calendar cards and guest-message posters), rockmywedding. co.uk and tinyurl.com/marthaweddings. You can also find some amazing personalised wedding prop ideas at notonthehighstreet.com.

Practical ideas can be great for decorating unusual parts of your venue too, such as a little basket of 'emergency' items for the loos containing spare tights, hairspray, paracetamol, blister plasters, chewing gum, Alka Seltzer, etc . . . These always go down a treat.

TABLE PLAN

TABLE 1

| TABLE 2 | TABLE 3 | TABLE 4 | TABLE 5 |

Table planning

Some brides and grooms find table planning the toughest and most argument-causing bit of wedmin. But it doesn't have to be. Just break it down into a few decisions: do you want to decide in advance which table your guests will be sitting on and exactly who they are sitting next to, or just have a total free-for-all? Next up, you'll need some practical info. How many tables will be in your venue? How many people will be sitting at each table? Would you like to have a 'top table' and, if so, who will be on it? Some brides or grooms with divorced parents or complicated families prefer to skip the whole tricky issue by veering away from a top table; others like to be surrounded by their entire family plus best man and maid of honour and have a formal, long table.

Sometimes the bridesmaids and best man are also seated at the top table, but some brides and grooms prefer a mini table just for two (most spend half the meal wandering around talking to guests anyway). And still other newly-weds prefer to sit with their best friends and seat their parents and close family next to their own good friends.

Whatever you decide, it is a good idea to make your choice early on in table planning so your venue or caterer knows how to set up the room, and you know how many other tables are available for your guests. If the dance floor and band/DJ area are moveable, and you're planning on having a kids and/or cake table, putting them on the table plan too will help later on.

Once all of your guests have RSVP'd you can – if you've chosen to – create the seating plan. There's the high-tech or low-tech option. Either way, you might want to give each set of parents their friends/guests/ relatives to sort out, leaving you with just the people you know best: much less of a headache.

The low-tech route is to jot down the name of each guest or couple on a sticky note, spread them out on a table or floor, and stack the papers of the people who 'go' together in groups of the number of seats per table. After the obvious people are done, you'll be left with a few people and can work out which tables still have room and who fits where. Or if that gets a bit messy, online table planning software could help. There are options you can pay for, but free ones are perfectly good: check out tinyurl.com/marthawedplan, where you simply upload your guest list and can then lift up names and place them at virtual tables arranged around the room. Or if you set up a wedding website (see page 186), some sites include table planning as a feature, so they will already have a list of your RSVP'd acceptances. Other sites offering free table planning software include tinyurl.com/tableplansoftware and ukbride. co.uk/table-planner.

Some brides and grooms are tempted to play get-your-own-back on people who've sat them next to Mr BO or near the loo on previous weddings with their seating plans. Or on that dreaded Table 9 with the work colleagues the couple felt they couldn't avoid inviting. You may face the dilemma of spreading your unpopular guests around the room, or lumping them all together in a table of boring relatives or dull colleagues. But be aware that the more smiling faces you see, the better your big day will be for you. And people are also likely to work out if you dumped them on Table Dull.

If you're inviting kids, sitting them on their own table with things to do can mean they're more likely to enjoy themselves than stuffed between grown-ups – but try to position the table out of the way of the dancing and away from the busy route that the waiters, etc. will take when carrying lots of food. There's no need to stress about everyone being seated next to people they know – it might not always be possible – but if you can, seat everyone *near* someone they know or at least a person you think they might get on with.

Once your plan is complete, some bridal parties like to get creative to reveal to guests where they're sitting. The easy option is to type up the table names and guest names sitting at each one in a list, or make an alphabetical list of guests with each table name next to their own name, and print it on A3 so everyone can

---

❝ I wish I'd thought of that …

Dafna married Jilpesh on Easter Saturday in 2010 near Bradford.

'My advice? Don't expect difficult relatives to get a personality transplant just because you are getting married. Just accept they will behave in an upsetting way and deal with it or take steps to avoid being near them. I think I would not have got as upset at my mother as I did if I'd been more realistic about what she is like, rather than imagining she would change just that one time. Get a good friend to confiscate your mobile phone the night before and screen calls . . . I ended up spending an hour calming down a distraught close friend who had just split up from her boyfriend, rather than the relaxing evening of pampering I had planned! Oh, and for God's sake, don't worry about the weather, there is no point . . . just hope for the best and buy some umbrellas from Ikea just in case!' **❞**

find their place. Escort cards are another idea – either traditional plain cards or imaginative ideas such as guests' names written on playing cards, matchboxes or seed packets.

Or you might want to go crazy with a creative idea such as guests' names on wooden sticks surrounding flowers in numbered plant pots, a chalk board with prettily written names, or even funny Polaroid-style printouts of pictures of your guests as kids/pulling stupid faces. You can find pics of these ideas and more at tinyurl.com/seatingplans. Or you could link your seating plan to your theme, like a cricket-themed wedding with miniature cricket bats each hosting a table-worth of names. Londoners could make a table plan like the Tube map and two scientists getting wed could use a periodic-table-themed table plan – see pictures of all of these ideas here: tinyurl.com/moreseatingplans.

Say cheese

How to find and what to ask for from a photographer/videographer

There you are, wearing the most spectacular clothes you'll probably ever wear, everything from your hair to your jewellery carefully planned, surrounded by your family and closest friends, riding in your dream car, in a cloud of bliss as everyone tells you that you look wonderful and passes on every wish for your happiness, and marrying the person you want by your side forever. And the closest way to bottle the feeling is by recording it in photos and video.

Not everyone feels thrilled about the paparazzo flash-bulb treatment on their wedding day. Shy or camera-hating brides and grooms might want a low-key snapper or just a friend to take some shots. But whatever you want, wedding photos are how you record your big day for posterity, show any future kids, and share the day with anyone who couldn't be there – and it's worth spending a little time thinking about who to pick to take them, how much to spend on it and what to expect.

James Tracey is a documentary-style wedding photographer who has himself just gotten married says, 'I've spent the last 18 months planning my own wedding – and know first-hand how difficult it can be to get everything organised and in budget.' After years of wedding-snapping experience – including one set of nuptials featured on *Don't Tell The Bride* ('mainly trying to get around the four-strong film crew who stole the best angles and gave me death stares whenever I fired my shutter') – James says nearly-weds should treat meeting a photographer as 'a job interview' for the snapper. 'Before you meet up, think about what you want from your photographer and prepare a list for your 'interview.'"

10 questions you should ask any potential wedding photographer

1. What's your photographic style?

'Most people have an idea of what type of photography they want,' explains James Tracey, 'they just don't know the name of the style or how to ask for it. Documentary or photojournalistic style involves working quietly in the background, catching the best moments without people knowing. A more traditional style involves a lot of posed couple shots and group images. Tell the photographer what you like and make sure they are comfortable with delivering it. Think about the kind of photos you've loved from other people's weddings and if possible have a couple of examples on hand on a laptop or phone. Establish how long the photographer will want to take posed shots of you during the day. Most brides and grooms like to keep their couple shots down to 20–30 minutes so they don't miss too much of their day.'

2. Can I see a full, sample wedding album?

'We've all bought a Greatest Hits CD, loved the songs and then gone and bought the latest album only to be disappointed by half of the album tracks – don't get caught out with your photos in the same way. All good photographers have their best images on their website – make sure all their photos in a whole album have consistently high-quality images,' says James.

3. What's your working day and what packages do you offer?

'Before you meet the photographer work out how much of your day you want them to cover. Do you want photographs from preparations through to the first dance? Are you only looking for photographs after the service and speeches? Some photographers offer packages where you can pick how much

10 questions you should ask any potential wedding photographer

coverage you want, usually by specifying a number of hours they will attend for. If you go for that option then you must ask what the additional charges are if you run late. I've yet to work a wedding where the timings haven't slipped. You need to know in advance if there's going to be an extra cost, and that the photographer won't up and leave when his time is up and you've not yet got round to that first dance!'

4. Do you do a free pre-wedding shoot?

'Unless you're a model, celebrity or an *X Factor* contestant,' explains James again, 'you probably won't be used to having a photographer follow you around for a full day. To help improve your chances of relaxing, see if the photographer offers an engagement shoot as a "test drive". It's usually done a couple of months before the wedding and is a great way to learn to relax with a camera chasing you about; and if you've any insecurities or you don't like a certain look or angle, this is the time to tell all.'

5. What happens if…?

'Test the photographer on what they would do if a mini-crisis develops. A good wedding photographer should have a little bit of Jack Bauer in them to make sure they can rise to whatever challenge is thrown their way – like how will they cope with a sudden blast of cold wintry weather? What will they do if their camera or lens gives up on them? Ask what insurance the photographer has. To work in most venues they will need Public Liability Insurance. But if they don't also have professional indemnity insurance, be wary. This covers them should there be a problem with their equipment or if the end product doesn't meet the standards you expect. It basically

10 questions you should ask any potential wedding photographer

means they are insured to cover financial loss should they have to pay you out for any reason. It's very important!'

6. Will you be photographing our day?

'This seems quite obvious but you won't have to go far to find someone who having met a certain photographer, had someone else turn up on the day. I'd run a mile if they said they weren't personally doing the work. Once they do confirm they are doing the photography on your day, ask what they will be wearing on the day. If you're organising a black tie affair, do you want someone in jeans and a T-shirt?'

7. How good is their customer service?

'Might be tough to ask the photographer this one, but you won't want to book someone who takes days, even weeks, to reply to emails and phone calls. So do some research – most photographers have Facebook and Twitter accounts. Watch out if there are Facebook pages where clients have been posting messages asking for their photos months after their wedding, with no reply from the photographer.

'There's nothing wrong with contacting some of the photographer's previous clients through social media either. Get a reference and ask the couples what they really thought of them. You're spending a lot of money, you should know as much as possible in advance about the person you're about to hand over your cash to.'

8. Do I have to pay for prints?

'The digital era has changed the way wedding photography works. Previously, in the film days, the photographer held the negatives and if you wanted pictures you had to pay for

10 questions you should ask any potential wedding photographer

re-prints. Now you'll probably want the photographer's wedding package to include all the high-resolution, post-production images on CD in JPEG format.

'Ensure the photos are high-resolution images: you want to be able to post online, print them, even use them to produce large products such as canvas prints. Check that you have a licence to print without any restrictions.'

9. Can we give you a list of photographs to take?

'Ask this to check the photographer's temperament and see if they would be open to collaborating with you. Be wary if the photographer says, 'Just trust me.' There's a fine line: you want a photographer who is going to capture the key details and the guests that are most important to you, while still giving them the freedom to do their own thing.'

10. How long until we get our photos?

'Some people take longer than others and this doesn't make them bad photographers,' James concludes. 'Turnaround time comes down to a lot of factors including how much post-production the photographer does and how busy they are at the time of your wedding. But experienced photographers will roughly know how long it takes to process your images. I normally say four weeks and then aim for two weeks. A month is reasonable.

'After you've met the photographer, the final questions are for you: Do we get along with them? Could we work with him/her all day? Do they get "us" and what we want? Do I love their style? If you can answer yes, you've probably found your photographer.'

> **I wish I'd thought of that ...**
>
> *Mother-of-the bride Ruth's three children got married within three years of each other.*
>
> 'We made a big mistake with one of the weddings of giving the photographer an enormous list of people we wanted photographs of, which delayed dinner until really, really late. I wished I had thought this one through.'

Money-saving photography

Wedding photography can cost anything from a few hundred pounds to several thousand. And it's difficult to compare photographers, price-wise, because they all offer different deals. Some might charge £1,500 for a day's unlimited snapping, a pre-wedding photoshoot, all the shots on a disc and an album too. Others might charge only £300 for five hours of footage, but by the time you've decided you want some extra time so they can record the preparations, and a little more so they're around for the dancing, and then realise you've got to pay extra for each print, the cost could spiral much higher.

Still, once you've decided on the style and type of photography you want, there are ways to cut costs. Wedding albums are very expensive, but you could make your own. 'If you are getting your images on CD (and you should be) then you can create your own album using one of the many online photo book companies like Bob Books or Blurb,' says James. For a small extra fee, Bob Books will even give you a professional designer to make the book for you once you've uploaded your shots.

You might also be able to negotiate extras (like pre-wedding shoots or parents' albums) for free. 'You only have to Google "wedding photographer" to see how many people are in the business,' James admits. 'If you've got as far as meeting a photographer, they would rather do a deal than see you go to a rival. Don't be afraid to ask for a discount. Be realistic, though: you can't expect someone to halve their costs, but there's no reason not to ask for 15 or 20 per cent off and see what flexibility there might be.'

The date of your wedding will have an impact on cost. Like venues, some photographers offer midweek and out-of-season reductions. 'Typically you can save around 20 per cent if you have a November to March wedding. Sure, it's cold, but we've not had a summer for years, so embrace the chilly weather, create a bit of the Blitz spirit and save yourself a bundle of cash,' James suggests.

Photographer Julia Boggio warns couples that you 'get what you pay for with photos', and advises brides on a budget: 'Don't skimp on quality, but see if you can tailor the package to what you can afford. If the photographer offers eight hours, see if you can have five (enough to cover from getting ready to the beginning of the wedding breakfast). Then ask all your guests to upload their photos to a common site, like PhotoBox, where you can make an album or prints of your own. Make sure that somebody captures the details of the day too, for example pictures of the flowers, your shoes, your dress and the food, as these images will help to breathe life into your album design and bring back your sensory memories of the day.

'You could also put your wedding photography on your gift list,' Julia adds, 'and ask guests to contribute (for example, they could buy you extra spreads in your album or a framed photo of you for the wall).'

James also has a high-risk money-saving suggestion. 'This one isn't for the faint-hearted and you have to be prepared to fail. The tactic is to wait. Most wedding photographers take bookings a year or so in advance. They know when they are working and when they aren't. If you wait and call them a few weeks before your wedding, providing they're available, you could get a massive reduction on the cost as they're unlikely to book another wedding with such short notice.

'We wedding photographers have mortgages to pay and kids to feed, so we'd rather have a booking every weekend, even if it is for slightly less. You have to be prepared for rejection, but create a list of 10 people you're interested in. Make sure you agree the total cost in advance, as some people may try and recoup their lower booking fee with extras added after the wedding.'

Alternatively, some brides and grooms prefer to opt for the amateur route. If you can't afford a professional, an enthusiastic hobbyist photographer could fit the bill. Don't ask Keen Uncle Derek just because he has a large DSLR camera – he could just have it switched on auto all the time, with little idea how to use it. 'If you decide to ask a friend then make sure they are good at taking pictures of people – taking photos of cars or landscapes is a totally different game,' says James. 'Or you could contact your local college or university. Most have photography courses and a ready-made bunch of people who lack real-life experience, but who have the knowledge and technical skill to take a decent photo. Students will have a portfolio for you to look at.

'Another place to search is Facebook and Twitter. When my band cancelled for my wedding, I asked for recommendations on Facebook,' James adds. 'I ended up with over 60 and booked a fantastic newly-formed five-piece band at a bargain price. There will be someone, somewhere, that will know somebody who is just starting out in the wedding business or who is a talented photographer. This does take a leap of faith but you could well save a lot of money.'

And a quick guide to posing from the photo experts. 'Many brides and grooms who come to me are worried about posing, as if I expect them to have the moves of a supermodel when I'm shooting them,' says Julia. 'Well, you can rest assured that your photographer doesn't expect you to be an expert in this. Good professional photographers know how to direct you so that you look your best. In my experience, men always worry about how their stomachs and chins look in photographs; women worry about how everything looks. I know I did at my wedding. Here are a few pointers on how to make different parts appear their best:

Chins – My mantra when it comes to chins is 'Look up!' Asking your photographer to take a few pictures of you from above will help to stretch out any extra skin, thus giving the appearance of a slimmer face.

Arms – There are a number of ways to hide arms. The easiest is to wear a wrap or a dress with sleeves. When being photographed, don't hold your arms close to your body, as this will only make them look bigger. Ask your photographer to help you pose your arms in a way that the camera will love.

Waist – If you're not happy with your waistline, there are tricks to help make it look slimmer. Look at yourself face on in the mirror. Now turn slowly to the side. Do you see how your waist starts to look smaller, or less wide, as you turn? Ultimately, you need to listen to what your photographer asks you to do.'

The video

Some brides are so film-obsessed that they'd have a 'making of' video documentary team following their wedding videographer if they could. But others worry about having a video – either because of the extra cost or because of having massive cameras shoved in their face and it all getting a bit too paparazzi-ish.

Videographer Adrian Stone offers his top tips on how to pick a pro, what to do if you can't afford one, and logistics on the day (see box).

What to do and ask before booking a videographer:

🖎 Watch at least 3–5 wedding highlights that they have filmed and edited to ensure you have an idea of their style and that you like it.

Carefully study their filming style: is it in a documentary style, with a focus on discretion, or do they direct you on the day? Ultimately, it is down to your personal preference as to how involved they are with regard to setting up shots and directing you.

🖎 If they are hands-on with directing, do they know/ work with your photographer?

Time is precious on a wedding day and it disappears very fast. If you have a photographer and a videographer both wanting to set up shots, you need to allow for plenty of time. A good rule of thumb is what takes 60 minutes on a normal day feels like 25 on your wedding day! Ensure that your videographer has a working relationship with your photographer, otherwise there could be a bit of conflict.

🖎 When looking at quotes from different videographers, check their coverage.

Ask how many hours they are planning to film of your wedding. To tell a great video story, you ideally need 12–14 hours of coverage.

🖎 Do you like them?

If your videographer does not come personally recommended to you, meet up with them to make

What to do and ask before booking a videographer:

sure you like their personality/character – they will be spending a lot of time with you on your wedding day.

🍃 **Are they lugging enormous TV-style cameras or something less conspicuous?**
Chat to them about the kind of equipment they use. Most of the younger guys are now filming with DSLR cameras which are small and discreet, and are great in low-light conditions. Some videographers are still filming with the big old broadcast cameras, which are very noticeable and need lots of additional lighting.

🍃 **Tried bartering?**
If you're on a budget, there is no harm in asking if they will do a deal for you. This is especially worthwhile if your wedding is in the quieter months of the year, such as October, November, January, February or March.

🍃 **Are you a pro, pro?**
Filming a wedding isn't just about the work on the day, it's also about the editing and the customer service they provide. Editing a video takes a good few days and is not something that can be done quickly. I average around 5–8 days editing a wedding video and always endeavour to have it finished within 6–8 weeks of the wedding. Ask your potential videographer how long they take; if someone has another full-time job, it will be a real challenge to fit the editing into their schedule and you could end up waiting a very long time for the finished product.'

The costs of wedding videos can vary enormously – upwards from a few hundred pounds to several thousand. It's not surprising that Adrian and his fellow pros advise nearly-weds to 'invest wisely in who you get to capture your special day, a thousand small moments that make up that one day,' but it is true that it's an area where you do usually get what you pay for.

Pro videographers use the latest gear – Adrian admits he carries £15,000-worth of kit around with him at a wedding. Perhaps more important than that, though, is that they know exactly what moments to look out for on the day. Adrian flags up 'when the florist arrives with the flowers to show the bride, always a great emotional moment to capture, or the moment when the bridesmaids and flower girls/page boys arrive and see the bride for the first time in the morning, and of course, the dad walking into the room and seeing his daughter all dressed up for the first time, the groom's speech where he talks about his wife for the first time and her reactions…'

But if your budget doesn't stretch, or you want a more casual video, another option is the hybrid route: pro equipment and pro editing, but your guests wielding the camera on the day. The idea shot to fame on the BBC's *Dragon's Den* show, where Shoot it Yourself (shoot-it-yourself.co.uk) talked about their business, which hires out broadcast-quality Sony video cameras to nearly-weds, tells friends or family how to film a wedding video, and then edits all of their footage into a professional wedding DVD with your own choice of music, titles and graphics. Its edited packages start from £849. Another provider is youfilmyourown.co.uk.

If you are getting friends to film your wedding, check that they are happy to be 'working' at your wedding instead of being a guest – no guzzling champers or socialising when they're meant to be filming. Adrian's other advice to pass on to anyone filming your big day without a background in wedding videos or recording is:

- Use a monopod and tripod and don't zoom in and out.
- For the video, capturing what people are saying is just as important as filming beautiful images. Break up the day into sections and make sure they get footage of each moment, from preparations, and guests arriving at the ceremony, to the ceremony, leaving the ceremony, the reception, the evening, speeches, dancing, the ending, etc.'

Did you know?

At wedding ceremonies held by the Masai tribe in Kenya, the father of the bride blesses her by spitting on her head and breasts.

What makes the best shots

What follows applies equally to your photos and video. If you're asking a friend or family member to take charge of taking snaps or the video on your big day, run through the points below with them, and even if you're hiring a professional it's worth talking through a few issues to avoid snags on the day.

Plan the official snaps to a T. 'One of the dads always goes AWOL at the time of the group photographs and it can take ages to round everyone up,' warns Adrian. 'I would highly recommend you have a bridesmaid or reliable usher who knows all the family members, to oversee rounding up everyone for the group photos. Even though reportage-style wedding photographers are now really popular, they are still required to do group photos – you might not want this, but your parents almost certainly will! My advice is to just bear with it and try to get it done as smoothly and as quickly as possible. It's not the time to be getting upset with your parents and/or those closest to you.'

Smile. 'Having a happy, cheerful couple who have let go of everything and are just enjoying their day regardless of anything makes for the best photos and video,' Adrian adds. 'I have seen too many brides, and occasionally the groom, getting all stressed and freaking out when things aren't perfect. This does not make for happy photos.'

Keep stress levels low; don't stray too far. 'Always try to get ready somewhere as close to the church or venue as possible,' says Adrian. 'Anywhere that requires longer than 30 minutes to get to the church could pose problems if you don't allow plenty of time for travel delays. Tractors on country roads, roadworks in London – they don't stop just because you are getting married. Drive around the block if you are on time, though – as there will always be guests arriving a few minutes late and you want them all in your wedding venue when you arrive.'

Aisle be there. 'My one bugbear at weddings is grooms who do not watch their bride walk up the aisle,' says Adrian. 'Because I know what is to come: the groom's speech, where he is going to say how beautiful you looked when he saw you walking up the aisle. And I'm thinking, No! No, no, no, you did not watch her walk up the aisle because the vicar said you should look straight ahead and watch him, and now it's on video which the bride is going to watch later on someday and want to question you over this little matter! Grooms, watch your bride walk up the aisle. It happens only once and ignore whoever is conducting the service if they say you must face forward!'

Don't forget the ending. 'The one thing I find couples never consider is how their wedding day will end. I always recommend having a strong finish and even though it sounds cheesy, making a tunnel, having sparklers, or asking the band or DJ to introduce a last dance with everyone standing in a circle around the couple always works so well for a memorable end. Even if you are planning on carrying on partying into the early hours of the morning, it's still great to have an official ending so that the older guests can leave and you can return, or carry on with the younger friends.'

Sorry to interrupt, but . . .

Insurance, loans and online shopping

Nothing in this chapter is going to make you squeal with pre-wedding excitement. No dress tips, no creative DIY ideas, no cake inspiration. But despite that, it could be the most important one you read, because there are some boring things here that need discussing, like the best ways to make purchases, how to protect yourself if a supplier goes bust and insuring your big day. All of these considerations could help save you huge amounts of money, and avoid an enormous amount of last-minute stress.

Before you spend a penny... get insured

At the start of wedding planning, most brides and grooms reckon there's no need for insurance because that's only for couples who are worried about one of them bailing out before the day . . . and that won't happen. But insurance is always a good idea whenever you're shelling out large amounts of money for something. It covers a huge range of potential wedding disasters, from your venue being flooded a week before your big day (it would pay for another one) to one of your suppliers cancelling on you and even your presents being stolen. And although, no one *expects* to be left at the altar, it's always worth insuring against this just in case.

One of the services some wedding insurers offer is counselling in the event that the big day does not take place. We all hope that will never be necessary, but the key things that brokers say you should include are:

- Cancellation
- Supplier failure

- Dress and attire
- Presents
- Photography/film
- Rings

How much you will want to be insured for, and therefore your total premium, will depend on the cost of your wedding. For example, if your rings cost £500, you'll need to insure up to that level, but if they cost more, you'll want to insure for more. Some policies are very cheap, and available for as little as £20, but these may be of little value if they don't pay out the sort of cash you would need to replace (or compensate for) any parts of your wedding day that don't go according to plan. One of the most important things to examine is the terms of 'supplier failure'. These are the main people you'll be relying on for your wedding service and reception.

You can compare of a range of wedding insurer rates and inclusions at tinyurl.com/whichinsurer, but do take some time to look into what you're covered for, including any excesses and insurance limits. Compare rates for your own requirements via a comparison site such as moneysupermarket.com/wedding-insurance, but not all providers may be included so look around independently too. Remember to look into policies particularly carefully if your plans have added complications, such as if your wedding is taking place abroad, or your reception and service take place on different days.

Wedding loans

A wedding loan should really be thought of as a last resort for brides and grooms. If you've cut all your costs to the minimum but still find you can't avoid going into the red then there are options for taking out short-term loans to help pay for the day. Like most nuptial services, mention of the word 'wedding' results in immediate price inflation. Google 'wedding loan' and you'll be sent to specialist sites offering sky-high rates. There are cheaper ways to borrow. If it's a little short-term borrowing you need, a credit card might be enough. Some offer interest-free cash worth thousands (depending on your credit score) for up to two years. The cards will allow you to pay back your debt over a specific length of time, without incurring extra charges, although you must ensure you can meet minimum repayments, or you'll face rocketing interest rates.

For smaller amounts, see if your bank will offer you an interest-free overdraft, which could give you access to £1,000 fairly straightforwardly. But again, ensure you are able to pay it back before the end of the stated term, as if you fail to do so, the interest rate immediately soars.

For those needing more cash, and potentially over

a longer period, a personal loan is usually the next-cheapest form of borrowing. The rate will depend on how much you need, and how well (or badly) the lender rates your credit score – that is, how reliable it thinks you are at paying back money. As a general indicator, however, borrowing, say, £7,000–£15,000 in this way will tend to see interest rates of between five and seven per cent. Work out exactly how much you'll have to pay back before taking out a loan via the calculator on the Money Advice Service (tinyurl.com/checkloanrate).

If you're being turned down for loans, or offered poor rates, check your credit rating for free via a provider like Noddle (noddle.co.uk). Read through the credit report, and if there are any errors, contact the credit reference agency to correct them or even explain any blots on your history. If, for example, you missed a loan payment because you were ill, ask your doctor for a note, and that will be added as an explainer on your report. You should also close accounts that you no longer use, join the electoral roll, and get a landline telephone to boost your rating.

Credit card payments

Even if you're able to foot the bill for your wedding in full, up front, it can still be a good idea to use a credit card to book suppliers and buy wedding goods because of the protection that doing so brings. Buy anything costing between £100 and £30,000 on a credit card, and the spending is covered by the Consumer Credit Act 1974, which makes card providers liable for any breach of contract or misrepresentation by the company. In plain English, what that means is that if you put, say, a £10,000 venue deposit on a credit card and the owner of the venue goes bust, or you order a £1,000 wedding dress from a supplier who suddenly disappears before its delivery, you can claim the money back from your credit card company.

Note that this guarantee only applies to purchases made on credit, not debit, cards. If you do find yourself needing to claim this way, consumer group Which? has a useful set of sample letters which you can use as templates for your own claims: tinyurl.com/whichletter.

Remember, though, if you are buying on a credit card, either use one of those mentioned above or, if at all possible, pay off the balance in full each month to avoid expensive fees and charges, many of which

are accumulative. If you are paying back the balance, use a credit card that offers extra rewards for your spending. Cashback credit cards – the most generous providers currently include American Express, Capital One and Santander – pay you back a percentage of your spending. When you're booking a wedding, that spending will quickly add up, and could maybe pay for a bit of your honeymoon. Someone spending £5,000 a year on a card paying out five per cent cashback on up to £2,000 spending for three months, then 1.25 per cent thereafter would pocket almost £100.

Bear in mind you have to pay off the balance in full each month to reap the rewards. It's best to set up a direct debit from your current account so you don't forget. Make sure you don't go above your borrowing limit – that will trigger punishing fees.

Shopping online

If you're buying anything online, take the following three steps to pocket major savings, which you can then put towards other parts of your wedding budget.

1   Compare prices via a price-comparison site, such as kelkoo.co.uk or priceinspector.co.uk.
2   Once you've found the site you want to purchase from, delete your computer's cookies – to make the computer forget where you've previously been. (Do so by clicking options/tools/delete cookies.)

3   Look online for a discount voucher. You can find these collated in one place via sites such as myvouchercodes.co.uk, or just Google the name of the product you want to buy or shop you want to buy it from together with the phrase 'discount code' or 'voucher code'.

4   Log into a cashback site – the biggest are topcashback. co.uk and quidco.com – and click through to the online store. Often, you will either get cashback or be able to use a voucher, unless the cashback site says otherwise. So work out which option would lead to the bigger saving, and use that to buy your item.

Most popular honeymoon destinations in 2012

Mexico	South Africa
Italy	Tanzania
Fiji	Seychelles
Maldives	Bahamas
Aruba	Florida

And finally...

Your day, your way

Among all the newly-weds who contributed to this book with their planning tips and advice, one comment cropped up the most. Whether they had wed in Britain, or abroad, in formal splendour or in Boho style, all brides and grooms lamented the same thing: it went by so fast.

And little surprise: however long you have to plan your big day, and whatever the style or budget, the build-up will probably start taking over your daydreams and nightmares, dominating every spare second and being all that your friends and family want to talk about. Then the day arrives and goes by faster than a rollercoaster circuit.

So when your wedding day dawns, if you possibly can, just forget about any worries, relax and enjoy it. Every second of it. Everyone will be wishing you their best, and your cheeks will start straining after beaming for 16 hours straight. To try to bottle the wedding day feeling, recent brides recommend taking a second out during the ceremony (preferably not when you're about to say 'I do') or reception to look around you, catch some eye contact with guests and drink it all in.

Some other tips? Forget about the agonised-over decisions about food or friends, and dance the night away. Dump your pre-wedding diet *immediately*, and relish every bite of the food you might well have spent ages deciding on. Oh, and catch a few minutes to talk to your new husband or wife throughout the day if you can, to let your newly-wed status sink in.

'The next day, reminisce a little,' adds a recent groom. 'On the morning after our wedding, my brother, who got hitched a few years earlier, advised my wife and me to take a few minutes to jot down memories of the day. We did so while mid-air en route to our honeymoon, and looking back now, only a few months later, that ripped-out page of memories brings back so much: my feelings when I saw my wife for the first time, our favourite music from the night, our parents' beams, my wife's jumping around in the morning when it became clear that it wasn't going to rain.'

Even if you've more video cameras filming your big day than on the average set of *EastEnders*, you can't beat a record of your own memories from what will be one of the most amazing and happy days of your life.

Wishing you huge good luck for your wedding and marriage. And enjoy the planning too!

Added extras A:
An Italian job

What you'll need for an Italian wedding

Nicoletta Caggiano handles the admin for brides and grooms looking to book Italian nuptials. As an example of the work involved, these are the steps she guides brides and grooms through to wed in Italy:

Nulla Osta – Certificate of No Impediment

In order to be married by an Italian officer you need to present a *Nulla Osta* (Certificate of No Impediment, issued by the Consulate) to the Italian authorities. This is the process you should follow to apply for such a certificate.

The first thing to do is approach your local Superintending Registrar and apply to give Notice of Marriage. Do this no sooner than three months before the wedding day. The banns will be posted for 21 days, and after that, if no impediments have been flagged up, the Superintending Registrar will issue a Certificate of No Impediment.

While you are waiting for the certificate, you'll need to collect the following documents:

- Full British birth certificates (the long version where both parents' name are recorded. The consular will not accept the short version).
- Passport details. (Check that your name on the passport is the same as the one on the birth certificate.)
- Passport details of the two witnesses – By Italian law you will need two witnesses at the wedding. Both

people will sign the register with you at the end of the ceremony. You can appoint anybody who is over 18 as a witness, however, please bear in mind that this is an important role so you might want to ask your bridesmaid or best man to do this.

Once the Certificate of No Impediment is issued you should send the documents below either to your agent or directly to the British Consulate in Italy:

- Original Certificate of No Impediment
- Original, full British birth certificates (long version)
- Copies of your passports (if possible, colour photocopies, otherwise make sure you send good and readable copies)
- Copies of witnesses' passports (again, if possible colour photocopies, but certainly they must be clear ones)

The agent will do an initial check and then liaise with the British Consulate in Italy. The latter, if all is cleared, will issue a Nulla Osta, which is basically the go-ahead to the Italian authorities for the celebration of the wedding.

Please note that by Italian law the civil ceremony will need to conducted in Italian, so if you don't speak the lingo then be prepared to smile and nod a lot. Alternatively you could organise for an interpreter.

Added extras B: The countdown planner

JULY

X	X	X	X	5	6
7	8	9	10	11	12
13	14	15	16	17	18
19	20	21	22	23	24
25	26	27	28	29	30
31					

From Yes to I Do to-do list

ASAP

Decide the type of ceremony you want.

Set the date with the officiants, your fiancé(e) and parents.

Call the people you really want to be there, or send 'save the date' emails or cards.

Set a budget.

Buy wedding insurance.

Decide on rough guest numbers (in order to work out venue options).

Choose your bridesmaids, best man, ushers and witnesses.

Research time

Visit and book ceremony at a church or other religious venue or register office, and/or reception venues.

Make appointments to visit dress shops.

Find a caterer, if there isn't one with the venue.

Book a photographer and perhaps also a videographer.

Visit florists to think about flowers, or choose other decorations if required.

Book your band/DJ/organise music.

If required, book ceremony musician/organise music options.

If you're going to pick a 'wedding colour' for invites/groomsmen's ties, etc., pick it now.

If required, look into transport options between ceremony and reception venue.

Start thinking about a honeymoon.

With six months to go you should:

Pick a wedding dress – six months is the minimum amount of time made-to-measure dress designers will demand before the big day.

Groom should buy/organise rental of suit.

Start thinking about, and making or ordering, invitations.

Pick outfits for bridesmaids and page boys.

If you want anyone else in the wedding party to wear a special colour/outfit, let them know now.

Finalise the guest list.

Book a hairdresser and make-up artist if required.

Book a Master of Ceremonies if required.

Four months to go

Choose buttonholes, bouquets and table centrepieces with florist if required.

Set up a wedding website – an easy and cheap way to give guests info, including accommodation details for out-of-towners.

Buy wedding rings.

Order wedding cake, if required.

Organise a hen/stag date with friends (and leave it to them to organise the rest!).

Three months to go

Register and choose your gift list, if wanted.

Finalise the menu and drinks choices with caterer arrange a tasting, if offered.

Discuss readings, hymns/music, and the style of service with your officiant.

Give friends/family who you want to be involved in the service readings/jobs, etc.

Order or make invitations and, if required, order of service, driving instructions, gift list insert and menus.

Book honeymoon, and check passport is up-to-date.

Buy any necessary extras such as veil, shoes (and a comfy pair for dancing?), tiara/headpiece, tights, underwear, garter for bride, and cufflinks, shirt and shoes for groom

If marrying at a church, organise the banns (see below).

Otherwise, contact your local register office (see below) to organise wedmin.

Two months to go

Send out wedding invitations.

Book a hair and make-up trial, if required (talk to a hairdresser earlier if you want to grow or drastically cut hair for the big day).

Organise meetings with each supplier (florist, photographer, venue, etc.) to finalise details.

Tell ushers and other members of the bridal party about their jobs on the day.

Write down all key phone numbers of suppliers to give to the venue or a member of bridal party who will be the go-to contact on the day.

Get any jabs required for honeymoon.

Buy/make any favours required.

Organise guest book, if required.

Organise any entertainment extras, such as kids' table activities, photo booth, etc.

Sort out any music song choices, and first dance song for band/DJ/iPod – plus selections for cake cutting, father/daughter dance, and last dance, if required.

Draft speeches.

Decide order of proceedings for reception – speeches, food/dancing, toasts, etc.

Make order of service/ceremony leaflet, if required.

One month to go

Once all acceptances/regrets received, order/make table plan or escort cards and place cards.

Buy any necessary gifts, e.g. for best man/parents/bridesmaids.

Contact each supplier to re-confirm booking, date and timings.

Organise final dress fitting and date for collection.

Organise first-night hotel room, if wanted.

Book any necessary beauty treatments.

Give final numbers and dietary requirements to caterer.

Finalise and practise speeches.

Organise someone to return any rented items after the wedding.

One week to go

Pick up dress.

Ensure all suppliers have been paid.

Take engagement ring into a jeweller to have it polished to sparkle.

Pack for honeymoon.

Wear in wedding shoes.

Finalise seating plan.

Write thank-you letters for any ordered gifts (you'll thank yourself post-honeymoon).

Put together an emergency kit (aspirin, make-up, hairspray, safety pins, spare tights, etc.).

One day to go

Decorate venue, if required.

Bride and groom: check all parts of outfits – e.g. for the bride: dress, tights, shoes, tiara, jewellery, etc.; for the groom: suit, speech in pocket, socks, shoes, shirt, etc. – are ready for the next day.

Ensure honeymoon suitcase is ready.

Get a manicure.

Relax…

Directory

Planning

General useful websites

confetti.co.uk – dresses, venues, honeymoons, inspiration and more

marthastewartweddings.com – huge US wedding site with real bride stories and resources

hitched.co.uk – mood boards, to-do lists, planning and more

theknot.com – another major US wedding site with resources, flowers, dresses and more

pinterest.com – scrapbooking site

youandyourwedding.co.uk and bridesmagazines.co.uk – wedding magazine websites with fashion, planning, hair and beauty

Lists, schedules and budgets

Online wedding schedules:
google.com/weddings/plan.html
myweddingdreams.co.uk/budgetplanner.php

Ceremonies

Practical info on UK weddings:
in England and Wales: tinyurl.com/CABwedinfo
in Scotland: tinyurl.com/CABscotwedinfo

Marriage abroad – Foreign Office info:
tinyurl.com/FCOwedinfo

Tuscan Dreams: wedding.tuscan-dreams.com

British Humanist Society: humanism.org.uk/ceremonies/humanist-weddings

Catholic Church wedding guide:
tinyurl.com/cathwedding

Church of England: yourchurchwedding.org/

Church of Scotland:
churchofscotland.org.uk/connect/life_events

Government marriage information: gov.uk/browse/
births-deaths-marriages/marriage-divorce

General register office for England and Wales:

gro.gov.uk/gro/content/

General register for Scotland:

gro-scotland.gov.uk/regscot/index.html

Jewish wedding links:
Reform: reformjudaism.org.uk/a-to-z-of-reform-
judaism/synagogue-life/wedding.html
Liberal: liberaljudaism.org/life-cycle/marriage-civil-
partnership.html
United: theus.org.uk/lifecycle/marriage

Methodist church: methodist.org.uk/who-we-are/
baptisms-weddings-and-funerals/weddings

Hindu: contact via temple

Sikh gurdwaras: nsouk.co.uk

Muslim: contact via mosque

Weddinspiration

These sites and blogs all host amazing real weddings
plus DIY projects and inspiration (UK and USA) – the
following list is basically how my computer's favourites
list looked before my own big day.
omgimgettingmarried.com
rockmywedding.com

whimsicalwonderlandweddings.com

diybride.com

wantthatwedding.co.uk

lovemydress.net

stylemepretty.com

belleamour.co.uk

beforethebigday.co.uk

onefabday.com

oh-lovely-day.com

theeverylastdetail.com

borrowedandblue.com

english-wedding.com – huge source of real weddings, divided by colour and season

Specialist wedblogs:

blovedweddings.com – a stylist writes about contemporary wedding ideas

mybigfatsponsoredwedding.com – as it sounds…

blog.african-americanbrides.com – black wedding site

southboundbride.com – South African wedding blog

hatunotblog.com – English-language guide to getting wed in Israel

thechiefbridesmaid.co.uk – budget-wedding ideas

bridesmaid.com – site made by dress group Dessy but still chock-full of ideas fiftieswedding.com – 1950s-style wedding days and ideas

weddinggowntown.com/blog – dresses galore

greenunion.co.uk and ethicalweddings.com – eco-friendly weddings

rocknrollbride.com – offbeat/alternative wed ideas

bridesupnorth.com – for brides in the north of the UK

apracticalwedding.com – answers practical wed-Qs

thebrokeassbride.com – 'bad-ass inspiration on a broke-ass budget'

adoreweddingblog.com – crafty DIY wedding ideas

Groom blogs

iamstaggered.com – groom? Stag? Father of the bride or groom? Go here (UK site).

groomsadvice.com – US blog with wed advice for the man going down the aisle

groom411.com – another US groom's site, with particularly good section on suits

groomgroove.com – speeches, guest lists, usher and best man advice, all wittily written.

Venues

Licensed wedding venues in England and Wales – searchable by area: tinyurl.com/wedvenues

Scotland: tinyurl.com/scotwedvenues

More venue search engines: weddingvenues.com
hitched.co.uk/wedding-venues
tinyurl.com/moreweddingvenues

Marquees: Stunning Tents stunningtents.co.uk

Wedding cars

Transport ideas:
hitched.co.uk/wedding-pictures/wedding-cars/
Wedding taxis:
londonblacktaxis.net/blog/wedding-taxis and
tinyurl.com/wedcabs
Replica TV and film cars: starcarhire.co.uk
Car confetti and decorations: carconfetti.co.uk/

Speeches

Advice: tinyurl.com/speeches101

Hundreds of wedding speech examples by grooms/
best men/brides/parents of the couple/maids of
honour: tinyurl.com/speeches102

Comedy bloke's speech advice: tinyurl.com/speeches103

More speech advice: tinyurl.com/speeches104

The dress

A to Z of wedding dress designs:
tinyurl.com/dressdesigners

Sassi Holford: sassiholford.com

Bridal gown sample sale lists:
bridesmagazine.co.uk/events

Once-worn gowns:
stillwhite.co.uk
bride2bride.co.uk
preloved.co.uk
sellmyweddingdress.co.uk
ebay.co.uk

Visit wedding shows to find inexpensive tried-on
dresses: nationalweddingshow.co.uk
designerweddingshow.co.uk
luxuryweddingshow.co.uk
nationalasianweddingshow.co.uk

High-street stockists:
Debenhams.com/women/dresses/wedding-dresses
John Lewis: tinyurl.com/JLgowns
House of Fraser: tinyurl.com/HOFgowns
TK Maxx: tinyurl.com/Maxxgowns
Charity wedding dress shops:
tinyurl.com/barnardosbride
tinyurl.com/redcrossbride and tinyurl.com/oxfambridal
Older brides, MotB: SoSensational.co.uk

Bridesmaids' dresses

Coast (coast-stores.com), Karen Millen (karenmillen.
com), Whistles (whistles.co.uk), Phase Eight (phase-
eight.co.uk) and Zara (zara.com)

Discount outlets: mcarthurglen.com/uk and
bicestervillage.com

Asos bridesmaid outfits: tinyurl.com/asosbridesmaids

Dessy: dessy.com/storefinder
Two Birds: twobirdsbridesmaid.co.uk

Bespoke maids gown: Maidstomeasure.com

Kids' bridesmaid dresses: perfumeriver.co.uk
debenhams.com/kids/occasionwear/dresses
next.co.uk/weddings
uk.monsoon.co.uk/uk/children/girls

Accessories

Wedding shoes: rainbowclub.co.uk/wedding-shoes
elegantsteps.co.uk/categories/Wedding-Shoes

splash-out Jimmy Choos (tinyurl.com/Chooshoes)

Bridal trainers/Converse: tinyurl.com/conversewedshoes

Bespoke shoes: upperstreet.com

Veils: weddingveilsdirect.co.uk and ukweddingveils.co.uk

Groom's gear

Ideas: bridesmagazine.co.uk/fashion/groom

Rental specialist: Moss.co.uk

Suppliers: hitched.co.uk/wedding-groom-attire/
mrporter.com/Shop/Clothing/Suits
tinyurl.com/debsgroom

Pretty details

Cheap spa days and treatments: Wahanda.com

Make-up artists quoted in this book:
Paula Kopitko (paulamakeup.co.uk) and
Robyn Alexandra (robynalexandra.co.uk)

Hair: Anna Charalambous of Angel Lounge hair
(angel-lounge.co.uk)

DIY dos: John Frieda's YouTube 'how to's'
tinyurl.com/johnfriedahair
easy up-do: tinyurl.com/weddingbun

Hair inspiration: tinyurl.com/pinteresthair

DIY details

(see wedspiration blogs below too)

Guest book ideas: tinyurl.com/weddingtreeprint
tinyurl.com/marthaguestbooks

Table name ideas: tinyurl.com/tableplanning

Table games: etsy.com/shop/KreativeCupcake

Props: notonthehighstreet.com/weddings

Kids ideas: tinyurl.com/confettikids

Kids crèche: artfullsplodgers.com
alittlesomethingextra.com

Favours: personalised Love Hearts:
tinyurl.com/ebaylovehearts or
shop.lovehearts.com/love-hearts

Personalised M&Ms: mymms.co.uk

Free printables:
offbeatbride.com/2012/06/diy-wedding-printables
(including DIY photo booth props, funny signs,
patterns for fabric bunting, 'just married' banners,
make-your-own cupcake wrappers, origami and
more)
weddingchicks.com/category/wedding-chicks/diy-
templates/; save-the-date calendar cards and guest-
message posters tinyurl.com/marthaweddings.

Table planning

tinyurl.com/marthawedplan

tinyurl.com/tableplansoftware

ukbride.co.uk/table-planner

Seating plan ideas: tinyurl.com/moreseatingplans

Seating templates: tinyurl.com/seatingplantemplate

Music

Wedding musicians: WeddingMusic.co.uk

Classic FM wedding music ideas:
tinyurl.com/classicfmwed

Ceremony ideas and music rights info:
pnms.co.uk/weddings/first.htm

DJ app: AccuBeatMix (wildbits.com/accubeatmi)

First dance inspiration: Anita + Patrick, with *Dirty*

Dancing's 'The Time of My Life': tinyurl.com/wedding-danceone

Andy and Kelly's mad medley: tinyurl.com/weddingdancetwo

Ryan and Frankie's jive: vimeo.com/41751468

hip-hop dance: tinyurl.com/weddingdancethree

First dance song suggestions: tinyurl.com/firstdancesongs and tinyurl.com/50firstdancesongs

Jazz Dynamos: jazzdynamos.co.uk and facebook.com/JazzDynamos

DJ James Regal: jamesregal.com

The cake

Wedding cake ideas: tinyurl.com/wedcakes
Cakes divided by colours: tinyurl.com/cakesbycolour
Supermarket option: (M&S) tinyurl.com/Markswedcake
DIY: tinyurl.com/wedcakerecipe
Alternatives to wedding cakes: tinyurl.com/altwedcakes
Personalised cupcake holder templates: tipnut.com/free-cupcake-wrappers

Booze

Work out how much alcohol you need per person: thealcoholcalculator.com

Booze cruise transport: ferrysavers.com
AFerry.co.uk

Wine clubs and online retailers: winesdirect.co.uk Virginwines.co.uk and majestic.co.uk (and branches)

Alcohol deals: quaffersoffers.co.uk

Cash 'n' carries: Costco (Costco.co.uk), Booker (Booker.co.uk) and Makro (store.makro.co.uk), Aldi (Aldi.co.uk) and Lidl (lidl.co.uk).

Invites

Invite inspiration:
ohsobeautifulpaper.com
tinyurl.com/marthainvite
pinterest.com/brideandjoy/amazing-invites/
tinyurl.com/inviteideas
tinyurl.com/inviteideas3
hobbycraft.co.uk/Pages/Ideas/
blog.weddingpaperdivas.com/

Free templates for DIY invites:
downloadandprint.com/templates/
tinyurl.com/invitetemplate
tinyurl.com/invitetemplate2

Cheap craft sources:
The Works (theworks.co.uk), Costco (Costco.co.uk), local craft stores and pound shops.

Online ideas: etsy.com
weddingcrafter.co.uk
handyhippo.co.uk

simplyribbons.com
fantasticribbons.com

Shop-bought invites: Marks & Spencer (tinyurl. com/MandSinvite), Paperchase (tinyurl.com/ paperchaseinvite), VistaPrint (tinyurl.com/ vistainvite), Confetti (confetti.co.uk), Hobbycraft (direct.hobbycraft.co.uk/shop/weddings).

Imaginative invite ideas: tea-towels: weddingteatowels.co.uk

Place mat and coaster: snapfish.co.uk

Personalised balloon invitations: customballoons.co.uk

Free fonts: dafont.com

Personalised invite/logo stamps: Stamps Direct: tinyurl.com/personalstamp
tinyurl.com/stampingallday
tinyurl.com/englishstamp

Letter costs: royalmail.com/price-finder

Invite wording samples: invitationconsultants.com/ sw-main.aspx

Wed-sites: mywedding.com
gettingmarried.co.uk
webeden.co.uk

Ceremony leaflet templates: tinyurl.com/ ceremonyleaflet

DIY leaflet-fan design: tinyurl.com/faninvites

Menu templates: tinyurl.com/menutemplate

Flowers

Flower inspiration: tinyurl.com/magflowers
myweddingflowerideas.co.uk
pinksweddings.com/wedding-flower-galleries/

Find once-used wedding vases and other accessories:
sellmywedding.co.uk

Picking flowers – what's in season/when: weddings.
co.uk/info/flowers.htm

Alternatives to bouquets: buttons or broaches,
feathers, clutch bags, fans, origami, sea shells:
tinyurl.com/altbouquet
tinyurl.com/altbouquet2
tinyurl.com/altbouquet3
tinyurl.com/altbouquet4
tinyurl.com/altbouquet5
tinyurl.com/dunelmsilkflowers
tinyurl.com/ikeasilkflowers
tinyurl.com/origamibirds
tinyurl.com/origamibirds2

Candles: candleking.co.uk
tinyurl.com/candleideas

Photos and video

Design your own albums: Blurb.com and bobbooks.co.uk

Guest photo upload sites: truprint.co.uk and PhotoBox.co.uk

Pro editing/DIY videoing: shoot-it-yourself.co.uk youfilmyourown.co.uk

Videographer in this book: Adrian Stone: thedreamcatchers.co.uk

Photographer James Tracey: jamestraceyphotography.com

Photographer Julia Boggio: juliaboggiostudios.com

Money and insurance

Wedding insurer rates and inclusions at tinyurl.com/whichinsurer

Comparison site: moneysupermarket.com/wedding-insurance

Borrowing advice: Money Advice Service (tinyurl.com/checkloanrate).

Credit rating check: (free) Noddle (noddle.co.uk)

Template for credit card claim: tinyurl.com/whichletter

Stockist shopping online

Price-comparison sites: kelkoo.co.uk or priceinspector. co.uk

Discount vouchers: myvouchercodes.co.uk

Cashback sites: topcashback.co.uk and quidco.com

Index

NOTES

NOTES

NOTES

NOTES

NOTES